D0820192

NATIONS
OF THE WORLD
CANADA

Greg Nickles and Niki Walker

RAINTREE
STECK-VAUGHN
PUBLISHERS

A Harcourt Company

Austin • New York
www.steck-vaughn.com

Steck-Vaughn Company

First published 2000 by Raintree Steck-Vaughn Publishers,
an imprint of Steck-Vaughn Company.
Copyright © 2000 Brown Partworks Limited.

Library of Congress Cataloging-in-Publication Data

Nickles, Greg, 1969–
   Canada / Greg Nickles and Niki Walker
     p. cm — (Nations of the World).
   Summary: Examines the land, people, and history of Canada and discusses its current state of affairs and place in the world today.
   Includes bibliographical references and index.
   ISBN 0-8172-5780-2
   1. Canada Juvenile literature.   I. Walker, Niki, 1972–
II. Title. III. Series: Nations of the world (Austin, Tex.)
F1008.2.N53 2000
971--dc21

                                                  99–42688
                                                   CIP

Printed and bound in the United States
1 2 3 4 5 6 7 8 9 0   04 03 02 01 00 99

Brown Partworks Limited
Project Editor: Robert Anderson
Designer: Joan Curtis
Cartographers: Joan Curtis and William Le Bihan
Picture Researcher: Brenda Clynch
Editorial Assistant: Roland Ellis
Indexer: Kay Ollerenshaw

Raintree Steck-Vaughn
Publishing Director: Walter Kossmann
Project Manager: Joyce Spicer
Editor: Shirley Shalit

Front cover: skaters on the Rideau Canal, Ottawa (background); crest poles, Stanley Park, Vanvouver (left); a *coureur du bois* (bottom right)
Title page: Peyto Lake in the Rocky Mountains

The acknowledgments on p. 128 form part of this copyright page.

Contents

Foreword

Since ancient times people have gathered together in communities where they could share and trade resources and strive to build a safe and happy environment. Gradually, as populations grew and societies became more complex, communities expanded to become nations—groups of people who felt sufficiently bound by a common heritage to work together for a shared future.

Land has usually played an important role in defining a nation. People have a natural affection for the landscape in which they grew up. They are proud of its natural beauties—the mountains, rivers, and forests—and of the towns and cities that flourish there. People are proud, too, of their nation's history—the shared struggles and achievements that have shaped the way they live today.

Religion, culture, race, and lifestyle, too, have sometimes played a role in fostering a nation's identity. Often, though, a nation includes people of different races, beliefs, and customs. Many may have come from distant countries.

Nations have rarely been fixed, unchanging things, either territorially or racially. Throughout history, borders have changed, often under the pressure of war, and people have migrated across the globe in search of a new life or because they are fleeing from oppression or disaster. The world's nations are still changing today: Some nations are breaking up and new nations are forming. At present there are 192 nations, as defined by the United Nations (UN).

Canada is the world's second-biggest country; it is also one of the most ethnically diverse. Many peoples have contributed to the formation of this relatively young nation, from the native peoples who have lived on its land for thousands of years and the colonists who settled there from the 16th century to the millions of migrants from around the world who have settled there ever since. Canada is a changing nation, too—some of its people are still deciding whether they want to remain as part of Canada or to form a new nation of their own.

Introduction

Canada is a vast country of spectacular landscapes. With a land area of about 3,851,790 square miles (9,976,136 sq. km), it is the second-largest country in the world after the Russian Federation and is larger than the United States, China, or Brazil. From north to south, it stretches down from beyond the magnetic north pole in the Arctic to the northern border of the United States; and from east to west, from the Atlantic Ocean to the Pacific.

Canada's only land neighbor is the United States. The two countries enjoy a friendly relationship, and Canadians and Americans are free to visit one another's country without a visa. The border is not guarded but has customs inspectors who search for restricted items such as illegal drugs. At more than 5,513 miles (8,892 km), it is the longest undefended border in the world.

The greater part of Canada is unspoiled wilderness. Most of the 30 or so million Canadians live in a narrow strip, about 185 miles (300 km) wide, along the Canadian–U.S. border. To the north are hundreds of miles of thick forest, rolling grassland, icy tundra, and towering mountains. There are roaring rivers and big, blue lakes, and the western coastline is a rugged fringe of fjords— narrow, steep-sided sea inlets—and islands.

A federal nation made up of ten provinces and three territories, Canada has its national capital in Ottawa. The country is also a constitutional monarchy: Queen

The maple tree is a national symbol of Canada. In fall its leaves turn golden, while in spring it produces a sap from which delicious maple syrup is made.

FACT FILE

- At its longest point, Canada extends about 2,700 miles (4,345 km) from north to south. From west to east, it is about 3,400 miles (5,472 km) wide, spanning six of the world's 24 time zones.

- Canada is one of the world's safest and wealthiest nations. Its people have a high standard of living and education, and they live a long time. Average life expectancy is 76.1 years for men and 81.8 years for women.

- Canada calls itself a "community of communities" because it is home to so many different peoples.

Canada's colorful dollar bills look unusual to many visiting Americans, who are accustomed to their green bills.

Elizabeth II of Britain is also Canada's queen. She does not govern the country but appoints a governor general to represent her. The federal government is run by the prime minister together with his or her Cabinet—a body of ministers, or state secretaries.

The currency system is based on the Canadian dollar—written C$ and comprising 100 cents. There are coins and paper money. There is a one-dollar coin nicknamed a "loonie" after the diving bird, called a loon, that appears on one face. The newer two-dollar coin is called a "toonie" to match. A portrait of Queen Elizabeth II appears on some Canadian dollar bills.

Canada's present national flag was first flown in 1965. Previously there had been a flag combining a shield of the Canadian Provinces' coats of arms with a small version

The Canadian flag has the national colors, red and white, and in the center is a stylized maple leaf, which is one of Canada's two national symbols.

of the British flag, the Union Jack, on a red background. This was called the Canadian Red Ensign. It was changed because the French-speaking minority in Canada did not want a flag showing a link with the British, who once ruled Canada.

In Canada people whose mother tongue is English are called anglophones, while people with French as their mother tongue are called francophones.

In addition each of the provinces and territories has its own flag (*see* p. 72 for example). The flag of Québec, for example, has a white cross on a deep blue background, with a white fleur-de-lys in each corner. The fleur-de-lys recalls Québec's historical associations with France—this stylized lily was the traditional symbol of French royalty. The Québec flag is an important symbol for Québécois (kay-beh-kwa) separatists—inhabitants of Québec who want independence from Canada.

POPULATION DENSITY

Some 90 percent of Canada's population lives within a narrow strip of land along the U.S.–Canada border, where the best agricultural soil is found.

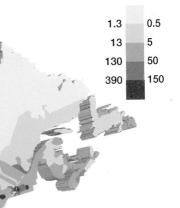

PERSONS

Per sq. mile	Per sq. km
1.3	0.5
13	5
130	50
390	150

LANGUAGES AND PEOPLE

Canadians have worked very hard to build a nation that encourages the preservation, celebration, and peaceful coexistence of many different cultural groups. Unlike the United States, where immigrant groups have always been encouraged to assimilate (blend) into the American "melting pot," Canada promotes multiculturalism. Its sizeable French- and English-speaking populations, together with its Native peoples, such as the Inuit and First Nations, and numerous other immigrant groups from around the world, have successfully held on to their traditional customs, beliefs, and languages. Some of Canada's cities, such as Toronto and Vancouver, are colorful patchworks of ethnic communities.

This graph shows how Canada's population has increased over time.

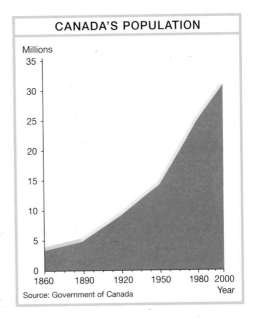

CANADA'S POPULATION

Millions

Source: Government of Canada

Year

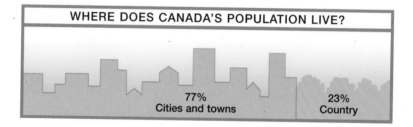

WHERE DOES CANADA'S POPULATION LIVE?

77%
Cities and towns

23%
Country

This chart shows that more than three-quarters of Canada's population lives in the cities.

These charts divide Canada's population by age, ethnicity, and religion.

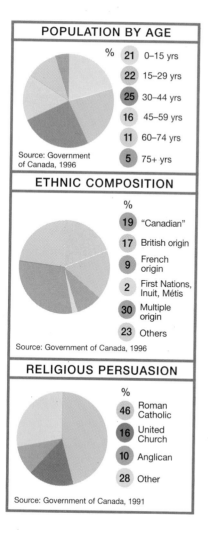

POPULATION BY AGE

%		
21	0–15 yrs
22	15–29 yrs
25	30–44 yrs
16	45–59 yrs
11	60–74 yrs
5	75+ yrs

Source: Government of Canada, 1996

ETHNIC COMPOSITION

%		
19	"Canadian"
17	British origin
9	French origin
2	First Nations, Inuit, Métis
30	Multiple origin
23	Others

Source: Government of Canada, 1996

RELIGIOUS PERSUASION

%		
46	Roman Catholic
16	United Church
10	Anglican
28	Other

Source: Government of Canada, 1991

Canada is one of the most sparsely populated countries in the world. Much of the country is unsuitable for settlement, so the population is scattered in clumps, separated by vast areas of inhospitable landscape. Some 77 percent of the population lives in cities and towns.

The country has two official languages: French and English. According to the census of 1996, about 67 percent of Canadians speak English as their mother tongue, while some 22 percent speak French. Many Native peoples continue to speak their traditional tongues, such as the Inuit language Inuktitut, in addition to English or French. More recent immigrant communities, such as the Chinese, Italian, Ukrainian, and Dutch, sometimes continue to use their mother tongue at home.

Many Canadians are bilingual—that is, they speak both English and French. Many signs in Québec are in French only. The French spoken in Québec—Québécois—can sound very different from European French. Local dialects, such as the *joual* spoken in parts of Québec, can be a mixture of 17th-century French, English words, and slang.

Just as there are many peoples and communities in Canada, so are there many religions. In Québec and New Brunswick, most people are Roman Catholic; elsewhere Protestant churches such as the United Church of Canada and the Anglican Church of Canada dominate. There are also many people who follow the Jewish, Greek Orthodox, Islamic, Hindu, and Native religions. Only a minority regularly attend some kind of religious service or observe religious beliefs strictly.

The National Anthem

Canada's national anthem began in 1880 as a French-Canadian song called "Chant national" (national song), composed by Calixa Lavallée (1842–1891). Canadians accepted the song for decades as the national anthem in preference to the actual anthem of the time, Britain's "God Save the King/Queen." The government officially declared "O Canada" to be the national anthem only in 1980. There are two versions of the anthem, one in French and one in English, which are quite different.

[British Canadian]
O Canada! Our home and native land!
True patriot love in all thy sons command.
With glowing hearts we see thee rise,
The True North strong and free!
From far and wide, O Canada, we stand on guard for thee.
God keep our land glorious and free!
O Canada we stand on guard for thee,
O Canada we stand on guard for thee.

[French Canadian translated into English]
O Canada! Land of our ancestors!
Your brow is barred with flowers!
For you bear both the sword
and the cross well!
Your history is an epic of the greatest exploits,
And your valor, tempered by faith,
Will protect our homes and our rights,
Will protect our homes and our rights.

No one really knows where the name "Canada" came from. The most widely told story attributes it to the Iroquois word for "village," *kanata*. French explorer Jacques Cartier (1491–1557) thought it was their name for the land around what is now Québec City. By the 19th century, the British used the term "Canada" to describe all the territories they still owned in North America after the American Revolution.

Land and Cities

"From sea to sea."

Canada's official motto

Canada's official motto—"From sea to sea"—reflects the fact that the country is bound by oceans on three sides. With the Pacific Ocean to the west, the Atlantic to the east, and the Arctic to the north, Canada's magnificent coastline measures about 152,110 miles (244,790 km)—the longest in the world.

Canada's coastline is highly varied. The Atlantic coast is rugged and windswept, with rocky coves and bays. There are sleepy old fishing villages of clapboard houses as well as big, bustling ports. On the other side of the continent, the mountainous Pacific coast is cut by deep fjords. However, around the modern city of Vancouver in the southwest corner of the country, there are sunny beaches. In the far north, the frozen Arctic coast is a rugged jigsaw of barren islands and desolate straits.

Water is also plentiful in the country's interior. Canada has 9 percent of the world's supply of fresh water, found in more than two million lakes and countless rivers and streams. The great St. Lawrence River is not Canada's longest river but is its most important. At its broad mouth on the Atlantic, the river is some 90 miles (145 km) wide. From there the river cuts deep into the Canadian heartland, stretching some 800 miles (1,290 km) to Lake Ontario and passing by some of Canada's most important cities. The river is part of one of the busiest waterways in the world—the St. Lawrence Seaway.

FACT FILE

- Canada sprawls across six time zones. When it is 11:30 P.M. in St. John's on the Atlantic coast, it is 11:00 P.M. in Halifax, 10:00 P.M. in Montréal, 9:00 P.M. in Winnipeg, 8:00 P.M. in Calgary, and 7:00 P.M. in Vancouver, on the Pacific coast.

- Canada is often thought of as a country of the north. However, Point Pelée, at the tip of the Ontario peninsula, lies south of 11 American states.

- Canada's longest river is the Mackenzie, which flows 2,635 miles (4,241 km) from the Great Slave Lake to the freezing Arctic Ocean.

Canada's cities are often separated by hundreds of miles of unspoiled wilderness. Here elk, or wapiti, wander in a mountain landscape in Manitoba.

13

THE TERRAIN

Geographers sometimes compare Canada's terrain to a vast basin. The basin's rim is formed by mountain chains to the north, east, and west but is broken by the lowlands of the south and northwest. The bottom of the basin forms the vast Hudson Bay.

Mountains, Plains, and a Shield

In the far west, the Coast and Rocky mountains run from the Yukon Territory in the north down through the provinces of British Columbia and western Alberta. Together the Rockies and the Coast mountains form the Western Cordillera region—a rugged area with jagged shorelines, tall, sharply peaked mountains, dense, temperate rain forest, and grassy plateaus.

The Coast Mountains rise steeply out of the ocean along the Pacific coast. They are the highest in Canada and include Mount Logan, the country's tallest peak at 19,850 feet (6,050 m). Their western slopes are covered with coniferous trees that form the only rain forest in North America, with the exception of southern Mexico.

The emerald-blue Peyto Lake lies high up in the Rocky Mountains. It is on the Icefields Parkway, a spectacular 142-mile (230 km) highway that runs between the Banff and Jasper national parks (see page 31).

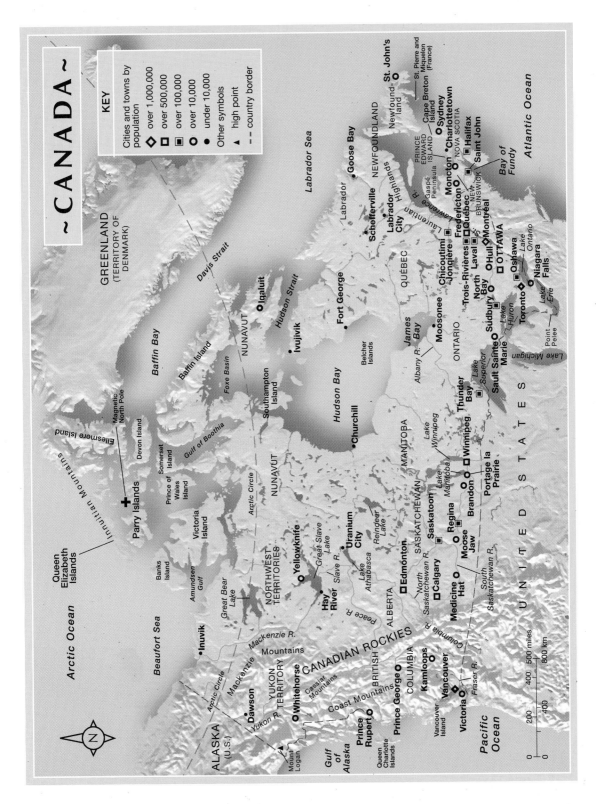

~CANADA~

The landforms that make up the Canadian "basin" fall into seven main regions, centered on the Canadian Shield. Some of Canada's landforms—such as the Interior Plains and Western Cordillera—are shared with the United States. The landscapes of each country flow into the other unbroken. Above the tree line, it is too cold for trees to grow.

To the east of the Coast Mountains are the Rockies. These form the main mountain system of North America and run some 3,000 miles (4,800 km) north to south from Canada to New Mexico in the United States. Between the Rockies and the Coast Mountains stretches a broad, rolling plateau of grasslands and smaller mountain ranges.

To the east of the Rockies are the Interior Plains—a vast expanse of flat and gently rolling land that includes the prairies. The region also includes wide river valleys, hills, and freshwater lakes. In the north the ground is frozen or marshy, while in parts of the south the ground is covered with rocks and sand dunes.

The Canadian Shield makes up about half of Canada. It is filled with low, rocky hills, swampland, thousands of lakes, and the largest conifer forests in the country. Its many rivers flow into the huge Hudson Bay. The

CANADA'S LANDFORMS

Western Cordillera
Along Canada's west coast are a series of mountain belts, including the rugged Rockies.

Arctic Archipelago
The Arctic Archipelago is made up of thousands of islands. In the far north are the snow-covered Innuitian Mountains.

Canadian Shield
This is the largest of Canada's land regions, covering almost half of its territory. It is made up of ancient eroded rock and forms a landscape riddled with lakes, ponds, and swamps.

Tree line

Hudson Bay

Tree line

Interior Plains
In the east of this region is the lake-studded Manitoba lowland, with an elevation of less than 1,000 feet (305 m). Westward, fertile plains rise gradually to meet the Western Cordillera.

Hudson Bay Lowlands
Toward the vast Hudson Bay, the Canadian Shield dips to form a largely forested lowland.

Great Lakes–St. Lawrence Lowlands
This small region is characterized by rolling, fertile landscapes. It is Canada's most densely populated area.

Appalachian Region
This region is characterized by low, rounded mountains. Lowlands are found along the region's seacoasts and river valleys.

Canadian Shield has some of the oldest rocks in the world, and these contain huge quantities of metallic minerals, such as zinc, copper, nickel, lead, and gold. On the southern coast of Hudson Bay is a smaller lowland region.

Much of the Canadian Shield is without forest. Trees do not grow in the permafrost—a permanently frozen layer that lies below the topsoil. This permafrost can be between 200 and 300 feet (60–90 m) deep. This bleak landscape is called tundra. During the region's brief summer, the surface of the tundra thaws enough to come alive with grasses, lichens, and brightly colored flowers.

This marshy, bleak landscape is typical of the Canadian Shield. Very little of this area is good for agriculture.

Lowlands, Lakes, and the Arctic Archipelago

The Great Lakes–St. Lawrence Lowlands region forms Canada's heartland. It contains rich farmland, important industries and is home to more than half of the total population. Its major geographic feature is a huge system of freshwater streams, rivers, and lakes that includes the Great Lakes. The Great Lakes form the largest body of fresh water in the world. Along with the St. Lawrence River, they are a vital source of fresh water for the millions of people who live in the region.

South and east of the St. Lawrence River, the landscape rises to form the Canadian basin's eastern rim. This is the Appalachian region. Here are very old and eroded mountains and, along the coasts and valleys, small areas of lowland.

The wild, icy Arctic region extends all the way to the magnetic north pole, which lies in Canadian territory. It includes many large and small islands, collectively called the Arctic Archipelago.

At 12,607 square miles (32,652 sq. km), the largest lake in Canada is the Great Bear Lake in the Northwest Territories. The Great Lakes do not count because they are all partly in U.S. territory.

THE PROVINCES AND TERRITORIES

Canada is divided into ten provinces and three territories. The provinces have a large degree of self-rule in matters such as education and health, and each has its own elected assembly and government. With the exception of the Inuit homeland of Nunavut (*see* p. 73), the huge and little-populated territories in the north of Canada are ruled directly by the federal government.

PROVINCES AND TERRITORIES OF CANADA

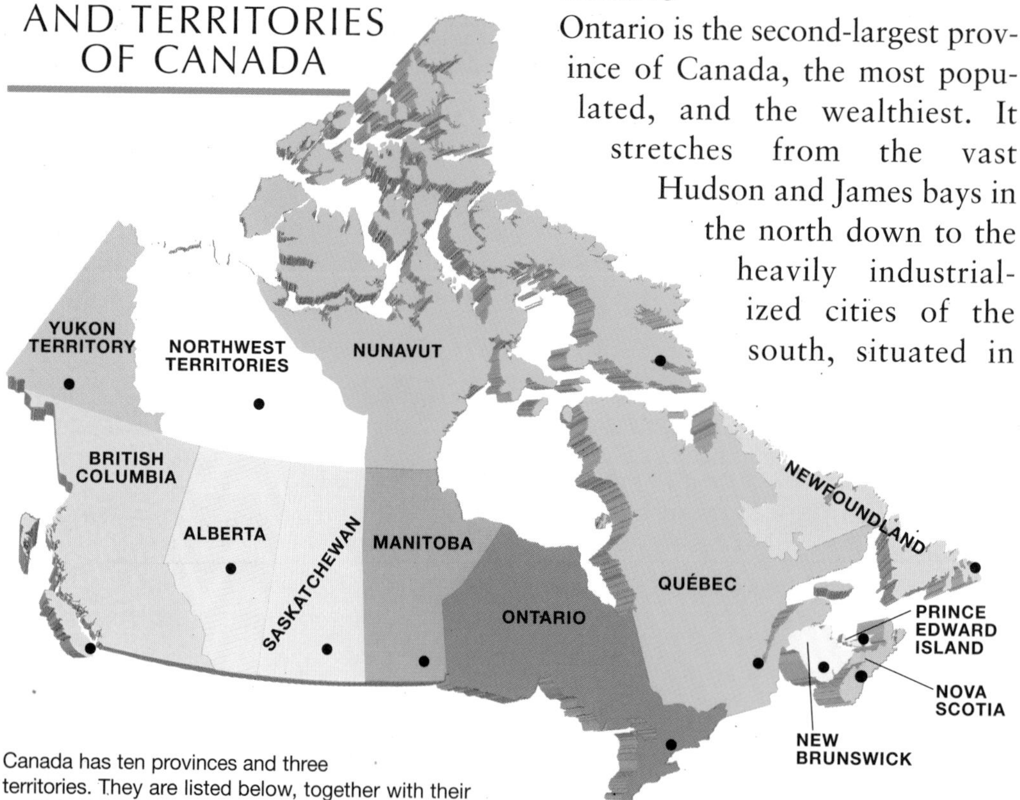

Canada has ten provinces and three territories. They are listed below, together with their capital, which is marked on the map with a dot.

THE PROVINCES
ALBERTA Edmonton
BRITISH COLUMBIA
  Victoria
MANITOBA Winnipeg
NEW BRUNSWICK
  Fredericton
NEWFOUNDLAND
  St. John's
NOVA SCOTIA Halifax
ONTARIO Toronto

PRINCE EDWARD ISLAND
  Charlottetown
QUÉBEC Québec City
SASKATCHEWAN
  Regina

THE TERRITORIES
NORTHWEST TERRITORIES
  Yellowknife
NUNAVUT Iqaluit
YUKON Whitehorse

Ontario

Ontario is the second-largest province of Canada, the most populated, and the wealthiest. It stretches from the vast Hudson and James bays in the north down to the heavily industrialized cities of the south, situated in the Great Lakes—St. Lawrence Lowlands. The provincial capital of Ontario is Toronto.

Northern Ontario is part of the Canadian Shield (*see* pp. 16–17). It is a rugged, wild landscape of lakes, rivers, and marshes.

Niagara Falls

The spectacular Niagara Falls lie on the border between New York State and Ontario. As the powerful Niagara River flows from Lake Erie into Lake Ontario, it plunges over a precipice to become Niagara Falls. The river is divided into two by tiny Goat Island. The falls carry 90 percent of the river's capacity.

The largest of the two waterfalls—the Horseshoe Falls—is in Canada and takes its name from the shape of the broad 2,200-foot (670 m) sweep. The clear, sediment-free water cascades 185 feet (56 m) in an awesome white sheet. The thunderous noise of falling water can be heard from far away. When Austrian composer Gustav Mahler (1860–1911) visited the falls, he is reputed to have shouted above the din: "At last, *fortissimo*." (*Fortissimo* is the musical term for "very loud.")

Over the years many people have performed daredevil feats at the falls. In 1860 Charles Blondin walked across the falls on a tightrope, stopping halfway to cook an omelette. Today the falls attract millions of visitors, who view this great natural wonder from every possible angle—from the surrounding parklands, from cablecars and platforms (as below), from bobbing boats, and even from tunnels cut into the rockface behind the cascade of water. Whichever way they choose, they are likely to get wet!

Québec's capital is the old and romantic Québec City. The city's most famous landmark, the copper-roofed Château Frontenac, towers over the mighty St. Lawrence River. The château, a hotel, is named after a 17th-century governor of the colony of New France, the Comte de Frontenac, who said of the city: "For me there is no site more beautiful nor more grandiose than that of Québec City."

Southern Ontario covers a much smaller area and is a fertile landscape of gentle hills and beautiful lakes. Before European settlement this region was occupied by the Huron, Erie, and Iroquois peoples. Because of the watery terrain, the Iroquois called the area Ontario, which means "glistening waters" in Iroquoian.

Unfortunately the dense population and heavy industry in southern Ontario have created serious pollution problems, particularly in the lakes. Many Ontarians are worried about the levels of industrial pollutants in the Great Lakes and poisonous mercury in northern lakes.

Québec

To the east of Ontario, on a great chunk of land half separated from the rest of Canada by the huge Hudson Bay, is the mainly French-speaking Québec. This is Canada's biggest province, making up a sixth of Canada's total territory. More than half of Québec is covered with forest and up to a million lakes and rivers. In the far north

is bleak, treeless tundra and taiga, featuring stunted, wind-blasted trees. The area is sparsely populated, mainly by Inuits. To the south lies the mighty St. Lawrence River. Between the Laurentian Mountains and the upper reaches of the river is Québec's most populated area. Here are two busy but contrasting cities. Québec City, the historical yet vibrant provincial capital, is Canada's oldest city and the only surviving fortified town in North America. Farther upstream is the great metropolis of Montréal (*see* pp. 36–41).

To the northeast of Québec City, the wild and lonely Gaspé Peninsula stretches out into the stormy Gulf of St. Lawrence. On its north shore lie the Chic-Choc Mountains, which are the highest in eastern Canada, and along its rocky coastline sit traditional fishing communities. Off its eastern tip is Bonaventure Island, a sanctuary for 25,000 birds.

New Brunswick

To the southeast of Québec, on a small rectangle of land between the Gaspé Peninsula and the U.S. state of Maine, is the Maritime (seaboard) province of New Brunswick. Much of its interior is covered with thickly forested uplands of pine, maple, and birch, and most of the population lives along the coastline or the rivers, such as the 418-mile-long (673 km) Saint John River.

To the south and west are the English-speaking areas, around the handsome provincial capital, Fredericton, and the much larger Saint John, an industrial port on the Bay of Fundy. To the north and east are the French-speaking districts that were once part of the French colony of Acadia (*see* p. 61).

Nova Scotia and Prince Edward Island

Southeast from New Brunswick is a forested peninsula, which is connected to the mainland by a narrow strip of land, and nearby Cape Breton Island. Together, the peninsula and island form the Maritime province of

Québec City took its name from a native word for the site, *kebec,* meaning "where the river narrows."

The oldest district of Québec City— *Vieux-Québec (Old Québec)*— dates to the 17th century. It is a World Heritage Site.

The province of New Brunswick gets its name from Brunswick, a dukedom in Germany that in the 18th century belonged to the British kings.

The Bay of Fundy, between Nova Scotia and New Brunswick, has the highest tides in the world. The water level can rise by as much as 70 feet (21 m).

One of Nova Scotia's most beautiful and most visited spots is Peggy's Cove, 30 miles (48 km) southwest of the capital, Halifax. It is famous for its boulder-strewn shoreline, its lighthouse, and its picturesque wooden houses and moorings.

Nova Scotia. In summer its wild, beautiful coastline attracts many tourists. The tiny village of Peggy's Cove is a particularly popular destination. In winter it can be bitterly cold. The early British settlers were nicknamed "bluenoses" because their noses turned blue with the cold as they fished.

The native inhabitants of the region were the Micmac people, whose Algonquian language survives in place-names such as Pugwash. For French settlers Nova Scotia was part of the settlement of Acadia. Scottish colonists, however, renamed it Nova Scotia ("New Scotland"). Nova Scotia's economy still relies heavily on fishing. The provincial capital is the big, busy port of Halifax.

The tiny, densely populated province of Prince Edward Island is joined to New Brunswick only by the 8-mile-long (13 km) Confederation Bridge, which opened in May 1997. The island's most famous inhabitant, Lucy Maud Montgomery (1874–1942), the author of *Anne of Green Gables*, described the island as "a green seclusion and haunt of ancient peace...with a fairy grace and charm." Prince Edward Island National Park has some of Canada's most beautiful, sandy beaches. The provincial capital is the elegant, tree-lined Charlottetown.

Newfoundland

Newfoundlanders call their remote and windswept island simply "The Rock." Newfoundland was first settled in the 16th century by a mixture of Irish and English people, who fished the great cod stocks of the Grand Banks. These are an ocean area to the southeast of Newfoundland. The unique identity of Newfoundlanders has been created by their ties to Britain (maintained until 1949), their dependence on the sea, and their separation from mainland Canada. Most people live in the port and provincial capital of St. John's, where many houses are painted in bright colors.

The rugged Newfoundland coastline is dotted with fishing settlements, called "outports."

Part of the province of Newfoundland is the wilderness of Labrador, a large slice of land that cuts into Québec. The North Atlantic Treaty Organization (NATO) has several airbases here and uses this area extensively for military maneuvers. The Inuit community of Labrador regularly protests against this use of its land. Labrador gave its name to a type of dog, the Labrador retriever, which was first bred there.

The *Dictionary of Newfoundland English* has more than 5,000 words. Most describe the weather, the countryside, or the local fishing industry.

The Prairie Provinces

In the center of Canada are the vast prairies that make up the provinces of Manitoba, Saskatchewan, and Alberta. Much of southern Manitoba is rich farming land. Farther north the landscape has the abundant forests and lakes typical of the Canadian Shield. The province is home to many Native peoples, such as the Assiniboine, as well as to Métis (*see* pp. 59 and 66). The provincial capital, Winnipeg, is close to the southern tip of Lake Winnipeg, which is the 13th-largest lake in the world. In the far north, on the edge of Hudson Bay, is the remote settlement of Churchill, once an important port. In summer people flock to the town to view the polar bears that come ashore here.

The province of Saskatchewan is very flat, and the landscape is dominated by its huge skies, with magnificent sunsets and sunrises. There are very few big cities and towns and little industry. In the northern part of the province there is a rich variety of wildlife, from wolves and black bears to mountain lions and grizzly bears. The provincial capital is Regina, which got its name from the Latin title of the British queen Victoria, *regina* ("queen").

The most western of the Prairie Provinces is Alberta, long the homeland of nomadic (roaming) Plains peoples, including the Blackfoot. The province has some of Canada's most spectacular scenery. Going westward the prairielands eventually give way to the awesome Canadian Rockies. The lower reaches of the mountains

The concrete-and-steel city of Calgary was originally a post of the Northwest Mounted Police (the Mounties). The city boomed in the 1960s when oil was discovered in the surrounding plains.

form Alberta's four national parks. The oil-rich provincial capital, Calgary, is similar to the oil city of Dallas, Texas, with soaring skyscrapers downtown and sprawling, low-rise suburbs. In downtown Calgary a network of enclosed walkways 15 feet (4.6 m) above street level connects many buildings.

British Columbia

Westward beyond the Rocky Mountains is the province of British Columbia. The province stretches through snow-capped mountains, forests, lakes, and grasslands all the way west to its fjord-cut coastline on the Pacific. The southern part of British Columbia's coastline is sheltered by Vancouver Island. It is the largest island off the west coast of North America, measuring 287 miles (462 km) long and between 30 and 50 miles (50–80 km) wide.

For some 12,000 years, the land was occupied by Northwest Coast natives, such as the Kwakwaka'wakw (*see* pp. 50–52). Today only Ontario and Québec are superior to British Columbia in terms of wealth and population size. The beauty of the region, its ski slopes and sunny beaches, and its mild climate and easygoing ambience, attract many visitors. British Columbia's capital,

Wheat predominates on the fertile plains of southern Alberta, Saskatchewan, and Manitoba. Other crops, along with livestock, contribute greatly to the economies of the Prairie Provinces.

British Columbia is Canada's third-largest province, covering more than 360,000 square miles (932,000 sq. km). It is larger than every American state except Alaska.

The Aurora Borealis

The northern reaches of Canada's provinces and territories are good places to see the atmospheric phenomenon called the aurora borealis, or northern lights. Fast-moving particles of energy (electrons) enter the Earth's atmosphere and are attracted to the polar regions' magnetic fields. There they react with atoms in the Earth's upper air to create a stunning display of shifting lights, usually colored green or red. Some Inuit believed that the lights were the spirits of dead ancestors or sacred animals. Gold prospectors (*see* p. 68) thought that they were the result of gases given off by ore deposits.

Victoria, lies on the southern tip of Vancouver Island, but the hub of the province is cosmopolitan Vancouver (*see* pp. 45–47), just across the strait on the mainland.

The Territories

Above the 60th parallel north are the vast, mournful lands that seem to stretch endlessly across the American continent—from the U.S state of Alaska to the island of Greenland and up to the North Pole. The Northwest Territories are

The Arctic Circle

In the northerly reaches of the territories begins the Arctic region of Canada. It comprises a fringe of mainland territory, bordering the often frozen Arctic Ocean, and countless islands, including the massive Victoria and Baffin islands. For nine months of the year, this landscape of low-lying hills and lakes lies icebound and in darkness. On Baffin Island, now part of the Territory of Nunavut, is Canada's second-most northerly national park, Auyuittuq National Park. In the brief summer, when there is daylight 24 hours a day, some tourists come to hike across the harsh landscape. Even in summer the temperature barely rises above 42°F (6°C).

the least-populated habitable regions of the world, and are the traditional homelands of the forest-dwelling Dene people and the Arctic Inuit.

The name "Yukon" comes from the Dene word for "great" and aptly describes its magnificent, lonely landscape of mountains and tundra. The region thrives on the tourists who come to trek through its unspoiled wilderness and on its wealth of minerals. Since the late 19th century, mining has been the Yukon's most important industry. The territory's capital is Whitehorse, once a layover for the Yukon gold-rushers of the late 19th century (*see* p. 68).

The Northwest Territories and Nunavut contain some of Canada's least accessible regions. The capital of the Northwest Territories is the city of Yellowknife, where most of the territory's 60,000 people live. In 1999 the eastern two-thirds of the Northwest Territories became Nunavut (*see* p. 73), the homeland for one of Canada's Native peoples, the Inuit (*see* p. 52). Its capital is Iqaluit, which is so small that it currently has no need for street names.

At 150,000 square miles (388,500 sq. km) Baffin Island in Nunavut is by far the largest island in Canada. It is twice the size of Canada's second-largest island, Victoria Island, in the Northwest Territories.

Canada's national animal is the beaver— a kind of river-dwelling rodent. The beaver uses silt, driftwood, and stones to build a dam in the river. The dam creates a large pond, which the beaver uses to protect itself and store winter food. At the same time as the beaver makes the dam, it also builds itself a den called a lodge. The grass-roofed lodge has two entrances—one on the riverbank and one under water.

WILDLIFE

The astounding variety of mammals, fish, birds, and other creatures that live throughout Canada is something about which the Canadian people are very proud. Their country's wildlife is portrayed on coins, in artwork, and in stories and poems.

The Beaver

The beaver is one of Canada's national symbols. (The other is the maple leaf.) Water-loving beavers live near Canada's lakes, rivers, and streams. They use their long, chisel-like front teeth to chew through branches and small tree trunks from which they build dams and lodges.

The beaver's thick, soft pelt long made it the prey of both Native peoples and later European settlers, for whom fur was a precious and very marketable commodity. Indeed, it was the demand for beaver fur in Europe in the 1600s that first led to the exploration and settlement of Canada by the French and English (*see* pp. 55–60). During the following centuries, the beaver was hunted almost to extinction. However, from the 19th century onward beaver fur started to go out of fashion, and the beaver population recovered. Today the Canadian government protects the beaver's habitats.

Omnivores and Herbivores

Bears are rugged animals that generally live in the wild, although the smell of food or garbage dumps sometimes attracts them into towns. The hardy black bear is the most common and is widely hunted. Its western relative,

The Seal Hunt

During the annual Newfoundland seal hunt, baby seals— also known as whitecoats—are clubbed and killed for their white fur. For a long while, the seal hunt, or cull, was a mainstay of the Newfoundland economy, providing both meat and an important source of income to the islanders. In the 1960s environmental groups such as Greenpeace began to campaign against the brutality of the cull. Glamorous movie stars, such as French actress Brigitte Bardot, gave their support to the campaign, and the environmental groups used disturbing images of the whitecoats covered in blood to promote the cause. The public outcry against the cull was such that the Canadian government restricted the number of seals that the islanders could kill.

The Newfoundlanders continue to be angry with this situation and argue that organizations such as Greenpeace— made up of people, they say, from the cities—have no right to interfere with their livelihood.

For the Inuit people of Canada's Arctic, seal meat and fur have always been crucial to their survival. In the new Inuit homeland of Nunavut, the people have the right to hunt seals without restriction. Here Inuit men skin seals they have killed, while a young boy tastes the fresh meat.

the grizzly bear, lives in the mountain forests of British Columbia. Polar bears are the largest land carnivores, or meat eaters, in the world; they live in the Arctic and can survive even the harshest cold.

Many types of large herbivores, or plant eaters, live throughout Canada. Some, such as caribou, musk oxen, and bison, live in herds that wander across the tundra and grasslands. Millions of bison once roamed North America. They were hunted almost to extinction, but about 8,000 bison now live safely in Wood Buffalo National Park (*see* map opposite), one of the largest nature reserves in the world.

Sky and Sea

Canada is the year-round home of many birds, such as the snowy owl and blue jay. In the spring countless other species visit to mate, nest, and raise their young. It is an especially popular summer stopover for many kinds of ducks, geese, songbirds, hawks, loons, and puffins.

Canada's waters and coasts are home to all sorts of animal life, including countless fish and crustaceans. Ocean mammals such as whales, walruses, and some seals visit during the summer, when the waters are warmest and food is most plentiful. Some kinds of seal live in the water even after it has frozen over in wintertime. These seals use holes in the ice to enable them to breathe. Whale hunting is strictly controlled in Canada because most species are endangered. The government, however, allows Inuit peoples to catch a few each year in order to preserve their traditional hunting skills.

The polar bear lives in Canada's Arctic region, but it can migrate as far south as the Gulf of St. Lawrence in pursuit of its main prey, the seal. The polar bear is a very good swimmer and is often found many miles from land. Since 1973 the polar bear has been protected.

Canada's National Parks

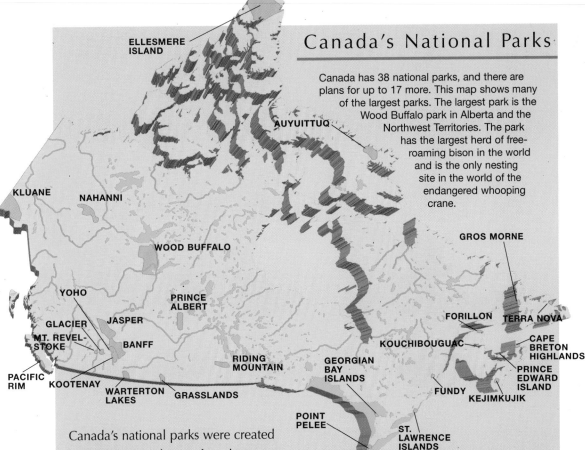

ELLESMERE ISLAND

AUYUITTUQ

KLUANE

NAHANNI

GROS MORNE

WOOD BUFFALO

YOHO

PRINCE ALBERT

GLACIER

JASPER

FORILLON   TERRA NOVA

MT. REVEL-STOKE

BANFF

KOUCHIBOUGUAC

CAPE BRETON HIGHLANDS

RIDING MOUNTAIN

PACIFIC RIM

KOOTENAY

GEORGIAN BAY ISLANDS

PRINCE EDWARD ISLAND

WARTERTON LAKES

GRASSLANDS

FUNDY

KEJIMKUJIK

POINT PELEE

ST. LAWRENCE ISLANDS

Canada has 38 national parks, and there are plans for up to 17 more. This map shows many of the largest parks. The largest park is the Wood Buffalo park in Alberta and the Northwest Territories. The park has the largest herd of free-roaming bison in the world and is the only nesting site in the world of the endangered whooping crane.

Canada's national parks were created to protect natural areas from human development and to teach Canadians more about the astonishing range of landscapes, plants, and wildlife in their country. Landscapes range from jagged Arctic ice (Ellesmere Island and Auyuittuq parks) and undisturbed prairie (Grasslands National Park) to majestic mountains (Banff, Glacier, Jasper, and Kootenay parks) and sandy beaches that are home to thousands of different birds (Point Pelée National Park). Visitors to these national parks enjoy a number of activities, such as hiking, swimming, climbing, and observing wildlife. The picture (left) shows the mountainous Banff National Park. Banff National Park is one of the largest of Canada's mountain parks, covering an area of 2,564 square miles (6,641 sq. km).

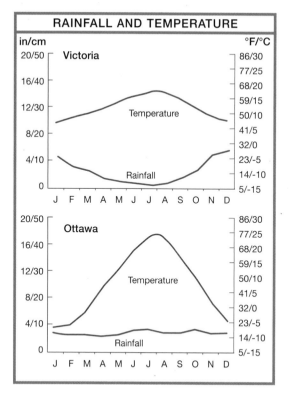

RAINFALL AND TEMPERATURE

in/cm — °F/°C

Victoria

Temperature

Rainfall

J F M A M J J A S O N D

Ottawa

Temperature

Rainfall

J F M A M J J A S O N D

CANADA'S CLIMATE

Canada is one of the coldest countries in the world. During the winter months, daily temperatures in most regions drop below freezing. Rivers and lakes freeze over, and storms blanket the land with snow. The mildest winters occur along the Pacific coast, where the cold weather may last just a few months, and rain falls instead of snow. Farther north the cold stays for half the year or more, and temperatures can fall as low as -40°F (-40°C). The northern Arctic is covered with ice and snow year round.

Different parts of Canada experience very different types of weather depending on their location and the season. Throughout the year Canadians must be prepared for all types of weather: from pleasant temperatures and sunshine to snow, ice, and freezing winds, to blistering heat and even hurricanes.

Although most of Canada's major towns and cities lie around the 50th parallel (50° North Latitude), they can have very different climates. Victoria, on Canada's west coast, has a Marine West Coast-type climate, with mild, wet winters and warm, dry summers. The capital, Ottawa, has long, cold winters, hot summers, and moderate rainfall all year round.

THE CHINOOK

During winter on the Interior Plains, spring temperatures can arrive within a few hours when a warm, westerly wind, called the chinook, rolls down the eastern slopes of the Rocky Mountains. Alberta's capital, Calgary, averages 30 to 35 chinook days each winter.

The chinook can raise the air temperature by as much as 18°F (10°C) in one hour and quickly thaws ice and melts away mounds of snow. The wind is named for the Chinook tribe near the Columbia River, in the direction from which the wind seemed to come.

CANADA'S CITIES

Canada has several major cities, some separated by long distances and sometimes rugged terrain. From west to east, some of the largest and most important cities are Vancouver, Calgary, Edmonton, Winnipeg, Toronto, Ottawa, Montréal, Québec City, and Halifax. Many of these cities are connected by the Trans-Canada Highway (*see* p. 91) that runs through Québec City on the St. Lawrence River to Vancouver on the Pacific Ocean.

Ottawa, Ontario: Canada's Capital

Ottawa, built on the bank of the Ottawa River, is home to the country's federal government. It is also said to be the coldest national capital in the world. In the 17th

Downtown Ottawa is divided into Upper and Lower towns. The Upper Town is set on a steep limestone cliff, while the Lower Town lies below, across the Rideau Canal.

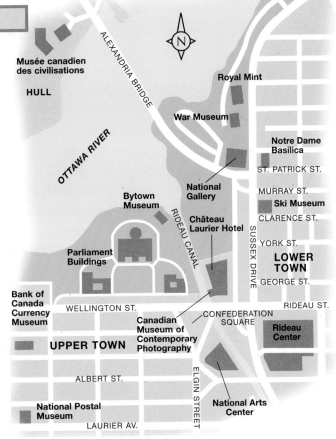

DOWNTOWN OTTAWA

Besides having such major museums as the National Gallery of Art, Ottawa also has many smaller museums that are well worth a visit. These include:

Bytown Museum
This tells the history of Ottawa from its origins as a workers' settlement to its current role as Canada's federal capital.

Currency Museum
This collection displays all the things that have been used as money in Canada, from whales' teeth, beaver pelts, and beads to modern banknotes.

Museum of Contemporary Photography
This has a collection of more than 158,000 photographs.

Ski Museum
In addition to a collection of skis and related equipment, this museum has a 5,000-year-old cave painting of men on skis.

War Museum
This has the largest collection of weapons in Canada. There is also a World War I trench and a car once used by Hermann Göring, a leading Nazi and friend of Adolf Hitler.

Map labels: Musée canadien des civilisations; HULL; Royal Mint; War Museum; Notre Dame Basilica; ST. PATRICK ST.; National Gallery; MURRAY ST.; Ski Museum; CLARENCE ST.; YORK ST.; Bytown Museum; Château Laurier Hotel; SUSSEX DRIVE; LOWER TOWN; GEORGE ST.; Parliament Buildings; RIDEAU CANAL; ALEXANDRIA BRIDGE; OTTAWA RIVER; Bank of Canada Currency Museum; WELLINGTON ST.; CONFEDERATION SQUARE; RIDEAU ST.; Rideau Center; Canadian Museum of Contemporary Photography; UPPER TOWN; ELGIN STREET; ALBERT ST.; National Postal Museum; National Arts Center; LAURIER AV.

The Canadian capital, Ottawa, has a beautiful setting overlooking the Ottawa River. To the right are the towers and spires of the parliament buildings. To the left is Alexandria Bridge, which crosses the Ottawa River to Hull, which lies in Québec.

The Rideau Canal links the Ottawa River to Lake Ontario. It was built in 1826 by Colonel John By, for whom Ottawa was originally named Bytown.

century, the Ottawa River was an important transportation route for the European settlers' flourishing fur trade. The name "Ottawa" comes from a Native word meaning "a place for trade."

In the 19th century, a ramshackle frontier city grew on the south side of the river, attracting a mixture of Irish, Scottish, and French workers. In 1857 the British head of state, Queen Victoria (1819–1901), chose Ottawa above its older and more established rival, Montréal, as the capital of the colony. Even today the city still has a small-town feel, and walking about its small, parklike downtown area is easy and pleasant.

Parliament Hill, where the government's legislative buildings tower over the Ottawa River, is the heart of the city. Canada's federal politicians meet in the parliament buildings, which are beautifully decorated with stained glass, marble arches, and gargoyles and surrounded by colorful flowerbeds. The National War Museum, Supreme Court, Canadian Royal Mint, foreign embassies, and many shops are all within walking distance of Parliament Hill. In winter the nearby Rideau Canal freezes over and becomes the longest skating rink in the world, more than 3 miles (5 km) long. Vendors sell hot chocolate and muffins to warm up the frozen skaters.

Close by are important national museums and galleries. Overlooking the Rideau Canal and the triangular Confederation Square is the National Arts Center, which houses theaters and an opera hall. In a bold, modern building, the National Gallery of Canada houses thousands of Canadian works of art. There are many important works by the Group of Seven, 20th-century Canadian artists who sought to capture in their paintings the vast landscapes of the northern wilderness (*see* p. 97). There is a rich collection of European and American paintings, too, including the well-known *Death of General Wolfe* (*see* p. 63) by American artist Benjamin West, as well as displays devoted to Inuit art. Beyond the National Gallery is Nepean Point, an area of parkland that looks out over the Ottawa River toward Hull (*see* box) and beyond to the Gatineau Hills.

Hull: Ottawa's Sister City

Connected to the capital by five bridges is Hull, Ottawa's French-speaking sister city, which lies in Québec. This former paper-milling town is chiefly famous for the spectacular *Musée canadien des civilisations* (Canadian Museum of Civilization), which stands on the waterfront. Native American architect Douglas Cardinal designed the museum to reflect the Canadian landscape as it changes from the forest and lakes of the Canadian Shield to the snow and ice of the far north.

This multimedia, "hands-on" museum shows the history of Canadian and other civilizations from the earliest times to the present day. There are full-scale models of the Viking landings in Canada (*see* p. 53), a French Acadian village (*see* p. 61), Pacific Coast longhouses, and a section of a 19th-century schooner (two-masted sailboat). In the Great Hall (*above*) is a large collection of totem poles.

North of Hull, and easily reached by bicycle, is the 88,000-acre (35,600 ha) Gatineau Park. Visitors to the park can hike or ski downhill or cross-country. They can also visit the country estate of William Lyon Mackenzie King (1874–1950) a former prime minister of Canada.

Montréal, Québec

Montréal—spelled Montreal in English—is built on a large island in the mighty St. Lawrence River. It is Canada's second-largest city and the second-largest French-speaking city in the world after Paris. Many of its inhabitants, however, speak English, and many are of Italian, Greek, Haitian, Vietnamese, or other heritage.

Geographically the city is as close to Europe as it is to the Pacific-coast city of Vancouver. It certainly is a striking blend of European and North American elements. New World skyscrapers of glass, steel, and concrete soar above Old World church spires, dormer roofs, and cobblestoned streets. A vibrant nightlife of restaurants

> In Montréal 70 percent of people claim French as their mother tongue, 15 percent English, and 15 percent other languages.

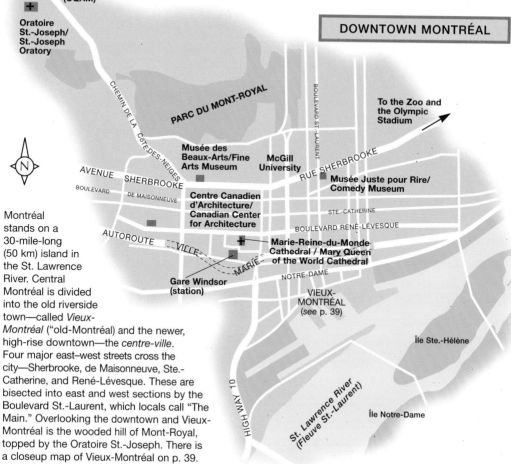

DOWNTOWN MONTRÉAL

To the Université de Québec à Montréal (UQAM)

Oratoire St.-Joseph/ St.-Joseph Oratory

PARC DU MONT-ROYAL

To the Zoo and the Olympic Stadium

CHEMIN DE LA CÔTE-DES-NEIGES

BOULEVARD ST.-LAURENT

Musée des Beaux-Arts/Fine Arts Museum

McGill University

RUE SHERBROOKE

Musée Juste pour Rire/ Comedy Museum

AVENUE SHERBROOKE

BOULEVARD DE MAISONNEUVE

Centre Canadien d'Architecture/ Canadian Center for Architecture

STE.-CATHERINE

BOULEVARD RENÉ-LÉVESQUE

AUTOROUTE VILLE-MARIE

Marie-Reine-du-Monde Cathedral / Mary Queen of the World Cathedral

NOTRE-DAME

Gare Windsor (station)

VIEUX- MONTRÉAL (see p. 39)

Île Ste.-Hélène

HIGHWAY 10

St. Lawrence River (Fleuve St.-Laurent)

Île Notre-Dame

Montréal stands on a 30-mile-long (50 km) island in the St. Lawrence River. Central Montréal is divided into the old riverside town—called *Vieux-Montréal* ("old-Montréal) and the newer, high-rise downtown—the *centre-ville*. Four major east–west streets cross the city—Sherbrooke, de Maisonneuve, Ste.-Catherine, and René-Lévesque. These are bisected into east and west sections by the Boulevard St.-Laurent, which locals call "The Main." Overlooking the downtown and Vieux-Montréal is the wooded hill of Mont-Royal, topped by the Oratoire St.-Joseph. There is a closeup map of Vieux-Montréal on p. 39.

MONTRÉAL MÉTRO

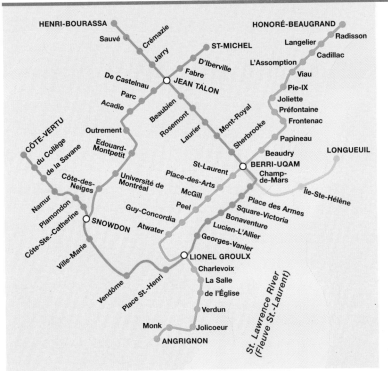

KEY

— Line with station

○ Interchange station

The best and cheapest way to get around in Montréal is by the Métro (the subway). It is modern, clean, and safe. There are four lines, each named after a color—Orange, Green, Blue, and Yellow—and 65 Métro stops. Each of the stops is decorated differently; some are worth visting just to see the station. The Place des Armes stop, for example, has displays of archaeological finds.

and clubs represents every part of the globe, and a calendar of cultural and street festivals (*see* pp. 109–111) ensures that no visitor is ever bored.

The island of Montréal was first settled by the Iroquois people, who called it Hochelaga, or "Place of the Beaver." In the 17th century, the French seized the island. Fifty-four men and women under the leadership of Paul de Chomedey, Sieur de Maisonneuve, founded a religious colony, which they called Ville-Marie ("the town of Mary") after the mother of Jesus Christ.

The colony grew quickly and became an important port for the French fur and lumber trades. After Britain overran France's Canadian territory, many Irish and Scottish immigrants flocked to the city, leading to tension between the French- and English-speaking communities. In 1837 there was a French uprising, which the British authorities brutally crushed.

One of de Maisonneuve's companions was the noblewoman Jeanne Mance. She founded the Hôpital Hôtel-Dieu de St.-Joseph (St. Joseph's Hospital), one of the city's major hospitals.

Despite these troubles the city quickly grew to become a bustling, lively port, with a reputation for an uproarious lifestyle and shady goings-on. During U.S. Prohibition from 1920 to 1933, Montréal provided the United States with much of its illegal alcohol.

Today's French speakers (or francophones) account for about 70 percent of the total population. They are intensely proud of their city and its culture. However, in the 1995 referendum almost 70 percent of Montréal's inhabitants voted against independence for Québec (*see* pp. 118–119). This is partly because most of Québec's English speakers and immigrants live in the city.

The island of Montréal is very large, measuring 30 miles by 10 miles (50 by 16 km). One of the best and most inexpensive ways to get around is by using the Métro (subway), which has four color-coded lines (*see* p. 37). The city center falls into two parts: the lively and largely high-rise downtown around Rue Sherbrooke and Boulevard René-Lévesque, and the charming Vieux-Montréal (Old Montreal), which runs down to the St. Lawrence River and the old docks of the Vieux-Port (Old Port).

Wandering along Vieux-Montréal's quaint cobble-stoned streets and alleys, or just sitting in one of its elegant squares, are pleasures in themselves, but there are many other fine sights to see. On either side of Montréal's oldest street, Rue Notre-Dame, are some of Canada's oldest public buildings.

Montréal's downtown is a mix of old and new. Here Christ Church Cathedral is dwarfed by a shiny new high-rise.

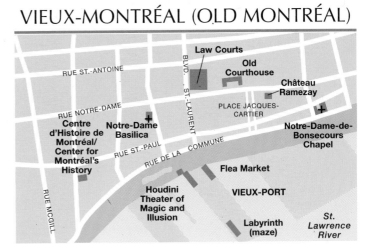

VIEUX-MONTRÉAL (OLD MONTRÉAL)

(map labels) Law Courts · RUE ST.-ANTOINE · Old Courthouse · BLVD. ST.-LAURENT · Château Ramezay · RUE NOTRE-DAME · PLACE JACQUES-CARTIER · Centre d'Histoire de Montréal/ Center for Montréal's History · Notre-Dame Basilica · Notre-Dame-de-Bonsecours Chapel · RUE ST.-PAUL · RUE DE LA COMMUNE · Flea Market · RUE MCGILL · Houdini Theater of Magic and Illusion · VIEUX-PORT · Labyrinth (maze) · St. Lawrence River

The impressive Notre-Dame Catholic Basilica (large church) dates from the early 19th century, though a basilica was first built on the site in 1643, the year after the first French settlers arrived. The church has two ornate towers, one of which houses one of North America's oldest bells. The bell is called Jean-Baptiste and can be heard 15 miles (25 km) away.

The Château Ramezay is older still than the present basilica, dating from the middle of the 18th century. Originally it housed the offices of the Compagnie des Indes (Indies Company), the company that ran the French colonial fur trade, but later it became the residence of the 11th governor of New France, Claude de Ramezay. Today it is an historical museum.

Close by is the lively Place Jacques-Cartier. At the center of the square is an empty plinth that once supported a monument to Lord Horatio Nelson, a celebrated British admiral. English-speaking Montrealers erected the statue to celebrate his defeat of the French at the famous battle of Trafalgar in 1805. The French-speaking Montrealers resented such an anti-French monument at the heart of their city, and the square has always been a focus for demonstrations, first against British, and then federal, rule. The statue of Nelson was taken down in 1997 and is unlikely ever to be put back again.

The shipyards of the Vieux-Port closed down in the 1970s and moved east of the city. Today the area has galleries, flea markets, a theater of magic and illusion, and a huge maze, which changes every week. There are boat trips available, too, along the St. Lawrence River and to the other islands that dot this great waterway.

The old town of Montréal runs down to the former docks. In Vieux-Montréal can be found many of the city's oldest buildings.

The Place Jacques-Cartier has many sidewalk cafés, called terrasses, and snack bars. Typical foods on sale include poutine (french fries covered in cottage cheese and gravy) and stimés (steamed hot dogs).

Historic Vieux-Montréal overlooks the St. Lawrence River. Rising behind is the business-dominated downtown.

The downtown area is not all high-rise buildings and street-level shops. There are numerous old churches, museums, and art galleries to be explored. The main street is fashionable Rue Sherbrooke, which runs halfway across the island of Montréal. The downtown district around Rue Sherbrooke was once known as the "Golden Square Mile" because of the concentration of wealthy people who lived there. Today the streets are lined with designer shops, luxury hotels such as the Ritz, and expensive apartments.

The Musée des Beaux-Arts (Museum of Fine Arts) is Canada's oldest museum, while the sleek, modern Centre Canadien d'Architecture (Canadian Center for Architecture) provides a fascinating introduction to its subject. Nearby, too, is the leafy campus of Montréal's famous McGill University.

At the very eastern end of Rue Sherbrooke are the Botanical Gardens, which include an insect-shaped building called the Insectarium that has about 130,000

The Université de Québec à Montréal (UQAM; pronounced *oo-kam* by francophones) is another important Montréal university.

insect specimens on display. Nearby is Olympic Park, home of the 1976 Summer Olympics and the futuristic Olympic Stadium.

Visible from everywhere in the city is the tree-covered "mountain" of Mont-Royal. Although Montrealers call it a mountain, Mont-Royal is just 738 feet (225 m) high and is an easy climb. The mountain is the symbolic heart of Montréal, and was named by the French explorer Jacques Cartier, who first visited the site in 1535. Today it is protected parkland, crested with a sanctuary called the Oratoire St.-Joseph (St. Joseph's Oratory, or just "St. Jo's") and a gigantic, illuminated cross. From the oratory are some stunning views back toward the city and the broad sweep of the St. Lawrence River.

Toronto, Ontario

The Toronto metropolis sprawls along the northern shore of Lake Ontario. It is Canada's largest city and also its center of commerce and communications. It is often said to be the most multicultural city in the world: There are communities of people from many backgrounds, including British, Portuguese, Chinese, Caribbean, Middle Eastern, Jewish, Italian and Vietnamese.

In early colonial times, Toronto stood at the crossing of ancient Native peoples' trading routes, a fact reflected in the meaning of the city's

DOWNTOWN TORONTO

In recent years the harborfront of downtown Toronto has been redeveloped, and today it has smart stores and museums. Ferries carry people to the Toronto Islands, where they can enjoy the cool lake breezes. North of the redeveloped harborside are the city's main business, administration, and shopping districts.

Casa Loma

DUPONT ST.

AVENUE RD.

BLOOR ST. WEST

Bata Shoe Museum

Gardiner Museum of Ceramic Art

AVE.

Royal Ontario Museum

YONGE ST.

CHURCH ST.

Ontario Legislative Building

SPADINA

COLLEGE ST.

BAY ST.

DUNDAS ST. WEST

UNIVERSITY AVE.

Art Gallery of Ontario

Toronto City Hall

Old City Hall

QUEEN ST. WEST.

KING ST. WEST

Gallery of Inuit Art

Hockey Hall of Fame

FRONT ST. WEST

SkyDome

CN Tower

Union Station

EXPRESSWAY

GARDINER

Ferry Terminal

Lake Ontario

N

Toronto City Airport

The SkyDome stadium stands in the shadow of the tapering Canadian National (CN) Tower—the tallest freestanding structure in the world.

name: "the meeting place." At the end of the 18th century, it was a tiny village and a military post, when the British chose it as the capital of their Upper Canada colony and changed its name to York. The difficult living conditions and uncomfortable climate earned it the nickname "Muddy York." In 1834 the city was incorporated and renamed Toronto; 33 years later it became the capital of the new province of Ontario. The site of the new capital proved a brilliant one. Its fine natural harbor connects Toronto, via the Great Lakes, to important U.S. ports and manufacturing centers such as Detroit and Chicago, and, via the St. Lawrence Seaway, to the Atlantic shipping routes.

In the 19th century, the city rapidly expanded, aided by the building of the Grand Trunk and Great Western railways and a commercial treaty with the United States. The downtown streets were laid out in a grid like New York's, and many grand municipal buildings were built. In 1851 the city's population was 30,000; by 1891 it was five times larger.

Despite this rapid expansion, for a long time Toronto kept its air of a conservative, provincial "backwater." Many people made fun of the city's supposed dullness, nicknaming it "Toronto the Good." Certainly its English-speaking inhabitants were very hardworking and lived quiet lives. One downtown department store even curtained off its showcase windows on Sundays to stop passers-by from indulging in the "sin" of window-shopping.

TORONTO'S NEIGHBORHOODS

Toronto is a city of many cultures. Over the years the various peoples who came here—Greeks, Italians, Chinese, Vietnamese, and Portuguese among them—made their home in different areas of the city. Today's Toronto is a mosaic of distinct districts, each with its own special atmosphere and heritage.

Little Italy

Toronto has one of the biggest Italian communities in North America, and little Italy is one of the liveliest downtown areas with numerous restaurants and food stores.

Kensington Market

This is a crowded neighborhood of narrow streets and colorful shops and restaurants. Many of Toronto's ethnic communities are represented here. In the market there are vintage clothes, fresh meats, French loaves and dark Russian rye breads, piles of fruits and cheeses, and spices from all over the world.

Nearby is Spadina Avenue, Toronto's widest street. This is another multiethnic area, where people come in search of bargains, from cheap designer clothes to glistening fresh fish.

Yorkville

In the 1960s painters, singers, and poets colonized this run-down area. There were jazz clubs, coffeehouses, and fashionable boutiques. Today the area is no longer as unconventional and is full of smart art galleries and expensive clothes shops.

Cabbagetown

In the 19th century, poor British immigrants lived here. In their tiny gardens, they planted row after row of cabbages to feed themselves—giving the district its name. Today Cabbagetown's Victorian cottages are more likely to be inhabited by prosperous Torontonians than poor immigrants.

Chinatown

There are more than 10,000 Chinese Canadians living in the city, and Toronto's Chinatown is one of its liveliest districts. People jostle through its crowded streets, which are lined with restaurants, bakeries, herbalists, and stores selling everything from electrical goods to porcelains, jades, and silks. Hundreds of Vietnamese also live in this area.

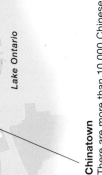

DANFORTH AV.

PAPE AV.

BROADVIEW RD.

JARVIS ST.

YONGE ST.

UNIVERSITY AVE.

CN Tower

EXPRESSWAY

Lake Ontario

SPADINA AV.

BATHURST ST.

BLOOR ST. WEST

QUEEN ST. WEST

KING ST. WEST

GARDINER

The CN Tower

The CN tower soars above Toronto's high-rise skyline. Visitors go up the tower in one of four glass-fronted elevators, which make the ascent at the rate of 20 feet (6 m) per second—roughly the same speed as a jet-plane takeoff. It takes just one minute to reach the top. Two-thirds of the way up is the Skypod, which has a revolving restaurant and a glass-floored balcony, from which there is a breathtaking view 1,122 feet (342 m) down to the ground. Higher still is the Space Deck. At an elevation of 1,465 feet (447 m), this is the highest public viewing gallery in the world.

The arrival of immigrant groups after World War II (1939–1945) and the setting up of large-scale government building programs challenged Toronto's reputation for dullness. Today the city is a lively, enterprising place with a jigsaw of ethnic neighborhoods that mirrors the multi-ethnic nature of Canada as a whole.

A visit to Toronto should include a trip to the Canadian National (CN) Tower (*see* box). At 1,815 feet (553 m), this is the tallest free-standing structure in the world. From the top it is possible to see along Lake Ontario as far as Niagara Falls and the U.S. city of Buffalo. Close by are the retractable-roofed SkyDome stadium—home of the popular Blue Jays baseball team—and the tall office towers of many banks and corporations.

Popular cultural attractions in downtown Toronto include the Royal Ontario Museum, which has displays of everything from dinosaurs and musical instruments to a lifelike bat cave with 4,000 freeze-dried or artificial bats. Nearby is the Bata Shoe Museum, which has a collection of more than 10,000 shoes from all over the world, including a pair of Elvis Presley's patent-leather loafers. Farther north is Casa Loma, a mock-medieval castle built in the early 1900s. The castle has secret sliding panels and passages, as well as some stunning views southward over the city.

Beneath the downtown skyscrapers lies the Underground City. Reputedly the longest pedestrian mall in the world, this stretches from Union Station in the south to Dundas St. in the north. In its 5 miles (8 km) of tunnels are galleries, fountains, and even trees.

The Vancouver-born architect who built Casa Loma, E.J. Lennox, also designed Toronto's beautiful Old City Hall. The futuristic new City Hall opened in 1965 on a site near the old one. It has a circular council chamber set between two curved towers. From above, the building looks like a big, open eye.

Torontonians enjoy visiting any of the countless restaurants, nightclubs, small galleries, theaters, and shops that reflect the city's many ethnic groups. They also love to celebrate the seasons of the year with large outdoor events such as the Royal Winter Fair, Santa Claus Parade, and the summer's Caribana Caribbean Festival and Canadian National Exhibition.

Vancouver, British Columbia

Vancouver, on the Pacific coast, is Canada's third-largest city and busiest port. It is also one of the country's youngest cities. It grew mainly after becoming the end point of Canada's first national railroad in the 1880s. The city was named in honor of Captain George Vancouver who, in 1792, was the first European to sail around Vancouver Island.

Today Vancouver is home to millions of people, including the second-largest Chinese immigrant community in the continent of North America. It has the mildest weather in Canada, as well as some of its most beautiful scenery. The city's skyline is dominated by majestic mountain peaks. Vancouverites and tourists alike love the city's mix of urban and natural scenery and activities. Sports fans enjoy events at the B.C. Place Stadium, while shoppers venture south by foot, bus, or ferry to Granville Island to wander around the public market and visit restaurants and theaters.

Stanley Park, not far west of downtown, is the largest urban park in North America, covering some

Everywhere you go in Vancouver are the sea and mountains. Here boats are moored in False Creek.

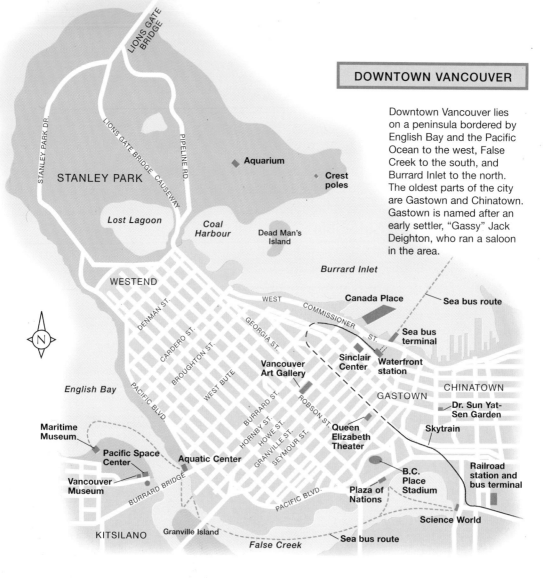

Downtown Vancouver lies on a peninsula bordered by English Bay and the Pacific Ocean to the west, False Creek to the south, and Burrard Inlet to the north. The oldest parts of the city are Gastown and Chinatown. Gastown is named after an early settler, "Gassy" Jack Deighton, who ran a saloon in the area.

LIONS GATE BRIDGE

STANLEY PARK DR.

LIONS GATE BRIDGE CAUSEWAY

PIPELINE RD.

STANLEY PARK

Aquarium

Crest poles

Lost Lagoon

Coal Harbour

Dead Man's Island

Burrard Inlet

WESTEND

WEST

COMMISSIONER ST.

Canada Place

Sea bus route

DENMAN ST.

GEORGIA ST.

Sea bus terminal

CARDERO ST.

Sinclair Center

Waterfront station

BROUGHTON ST.

Vancouver Art Gallery

English Bay

WEST BUTE

PACIFIC BLVD.

BURRARD ST.

ROBSON ST.

GASTOWN

CHINATOWN

Dr. Sun Yat-Sen Garden

Maritime Museum

HORNBY ST.

HOWE ST.

Queen Elizabeth Theater

Skytrain

Pacific Space Center

Aquatic Center

GRANVILLE ST.

SEYMOUR ST.

Railroad station and bus terminal

Vancouver Museum

BURRARD BRIDGE

Plaza of Nations

B.C. Place Stadium

Science World

PACIFIC BLVD.

KITSILANO

Granville Island

False Creek

Sea bus route

1,000 acres (400 ha). It offers woodlands, beaches, and boating. This semi-wilderness features totem pole displays (*see* pp. 50 and 96–97) and the Vancouver Public Aquarium, which houses orcas, beluga whales, and many other sea creatures. Hikers and skiers often travel a little way east of the city for the slopes of the Coast Mountains.

Seasonal events include the Abbotsford Air Show, the largest in North America, and the annual winter Polar Bear swim, during which hundreds of people plunge into the cold ocean. The Chinese New Year is celebrated in Vancouver's vibrant Chinatown in January or February with a Dragon Parade and other festivities.

Vancouver's Chinatown

Vancouver's large Chinese community first developed during the gold rushes of the 19th century (*see* p. 68). The British majority population treated the new immigrants badly: The Chinese gained Canadian citizenship only in 1947. Rejected by mainstream society, the community built its own neighborhood where the Chinese could feel comfortable.

Today Chinatown is one of the most vibrant areas of Vancouver. Its traditional Chinese architecture of ornamental roofs and colorful balconies and its busy markets (*below*) provide an authentic and exhilarating experience of traditional Chinese life. The items for sale include live eels, sweet-bean buns and moon cakes, fragrant teas, and medicines such as dried sea horses and buffalo tongues.

After the bustle of street life, visitors can find an opportunity for peace and contemplation in Dr. Sun Yat-Sen Garden. In this traditional Chinese garden, stones and flowers are carefully arranged to bring the Taoist forces of yin and yang into complete harmony.

Past and Present

"The somber but august grandeur of the forces that hemmed us in...soon cast their magic spell upon our spirits, and we began to feel charmed with the freedom and solitude around us."

British emigrant to Canada Susannah Moodie (1803–1885)

Canada, like its neighbor, the United States, is a relatively young nation. It was founded only in 1867, and although it was largely self-governed, it was not until 1931 that Britain granted Canada official independence. Nevertheless, the story of this vast territory stretches back thousands of years and has been shaped by many peoples—from the First Nations and Inuit peoples who settled the country thousands of years ago to more recent settlers from Europe, the United States, and many other countries. Even the name "Canada" was accepted as the country's name only in 1867.

Throughout their country's history, the various Canadian peoples have had to overcome the daunting obstacles presented by the Canadian wilderness. Native and other minority peoples have also had to struggle to maintain their unique cultures as those of dominant peoples, of colonial powers such as France and Britain, and of the United States have threatened to overwhelm them.

The diversity of its peoples and the vastness of its landscape have meant that Canada has strong regional identities. Often this regionalism has led to a spirit of compromise and collaboration—as shown in the recent creation of a new homeland for the Inuit, called Nunavut ("our land"). Sometimes—as today with the Québec separatist movement—it has threatened to tear the country apart.

A 16th-century French map shows Jacques Cartier landing on the banks of the St. Lawrence River, here called the Rio do Canada ("river of Canada").

FACT FILE

● In the 16th century, the name *Canada* was used to refer to the land along the St. Lawrence River near present-day Québec City. Later it became another name for the colony of New France. After 1867 the word was given to the new confederation of British colonies in North America.

● Canada was a European colony for more than 300 years, from the foundation of Port Royal in 1605 to full independence in 1931.

● Today Canada plays an important part in international relations. It is a founding member of the United Nations (UN) and is an active peacekeeper in many UN operations.

CANADA'S FIRST PEOPLES

Experts believe that people have lived in North America for more than 30,000 years. The first peoples probably came from northeastern Asia by way of a giant land bridge that once connected Siberia and Alaska. When the sea level rose to cover the land bridge, the area became the channel of water known as the Bering Strait.

The newcomers gradually made their way throughout the Americas in search of hunting grounds. As they migrated across the continent, they adapted to the different types of land and climate they found. Over thousands of years, different groups developed, each with its own distinctive culture and language. These groups included the Maya, Inca, and Aztecs who founded the civilizations of Mexico and Central and South America as well as the numerous Native peoples of North America.

Those peoples who settled in what is today Canada are known as the First Nations. The Inuit peoples who settled in Canada's Arctic regions arrived in the North American continent later than other Native peoples—perhaps about 4,000 years ago.

A Diversity of Cultures

Canada's extremely varied landscape and climate gave rise to widely differing ways of life (*see* map opposite). Two of the most famous peoples of Canada are the Kwakwaka'wakw (or Kwakiutl) and Inuit. The Kwakwaka'-wakw people traditionally lived on the shores of what is today Vancouver Island and the nearby mainland. In the summer months, they were usually nomadic, but in winter they lived close to the seashore in family dwellings made

The Kwakwaka-wakw people of present-day British Columbia are highly skilled woodworkers. Among their most impressive achievements are magnificent, brilliantly colored crest ("totem") poles carved out of cedarwood. These crest poles below stand in Stanley Park in Vancouver.

Who Were Canada's First Peoples?

The earliest inhabitants of what is now Canada came from Asia, crossing into North America some 30,000 years ago. From Alaska they spread throughout the continent, adapting to the environmental conditions they found. Scholars divide North American peoples into broad cultural groups that follow the continent's geographic areas. In Canada there are Arctic, Subarctic, Northwest Coast, Plateau, Plains, and Eastern Woodland groups. In the map below, the words in capitals are the names of some the most important tribes.

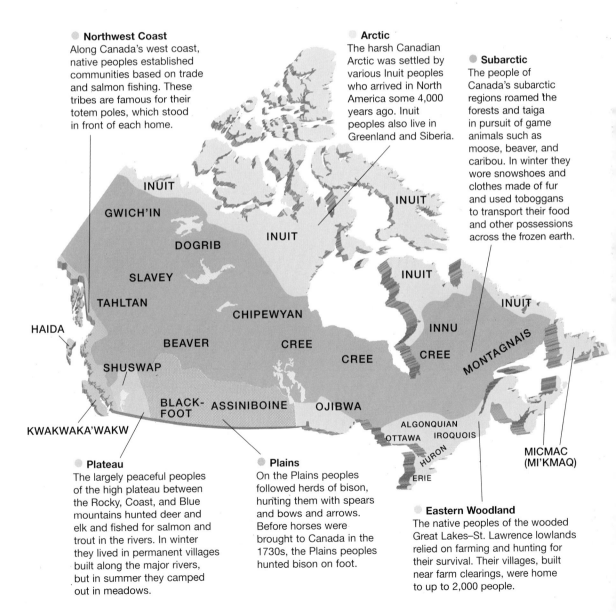

● Northwest Coast
Along Canada's west coast, native peoples established communities based on trade and salmon fishing. These tribes are famous for their totem poles, which stood in front of each home.

● Arctic
The harsh Canadian Arctic was settled by various Inuit peoples who arrived in North America some 4,000 years ago. Inuit peoples also live in Greenland and Siberia.

● Subarctic
The people of Canada's subarctic regions roamed the forests and taiga in pursuit of game animals such as moose, beaver, and caribou. In winter they wore snowshoes and clothes made of fur and used toboggans to transport their food and other possessions across the frozen earth.

INUIT
GWICH'IN
DOGRIB
INUIT
SLAVEY
INUIT
TAHLTAN
INUIT
HAIDA
CHIPEWYAN
INNU
BEAVER
CREE
CREE
MONTAGNAIS
SHUSWAP
CREE
BLACK-FOOT
ASSINIBOINE
OJIBWA
KWAKWAKA'WAKW
ALGONQUIAN
OTTAWA
IROQUOIS
HURON
MICMAC (MI'KMAQ)
ERIE

● Plateau
The largely peaceful peoples of the high plateau between the Rocky, Coast, and Blue mountains hunted deer and elk and fished for salmon and trout in the rivers. In winter they lived in permanent villages built along the major rivers, but in summer they camped out in meadows.

● Plains
On the Plains peoples followed herds of bison, hunting them with spears and bows and arrows. Before horses were brought to Canada in the 1730s, the Plains peoples hunted bison on foot.

● Eastern Woodland
The native peoples of the wooded Great Lakes–St. Lawrence lowlands relied on farming and hunting for their survival. Their villages, built near farm clearings, were home to up to 2,000 people.

*A 19th-century
European illustration
shows the Inuit
of Labrador. The
Europeans called
the Arctic peoples
of Canada "Eskimos,"
a word that may
mean "meateaters."*

out of cedarwood. They carved tall cedarwood crest, or "totem," poles, which they often placed on the beachfront to greet visitors (*see* pp. 96–97). The Kwakwaka'wakw were expert fishermen, using harpoons to hunt whales. They were also tireless traders, bartering copper, seashells, decorated pots, and patterned blankets.

Kwakwaka'wakw society, like that of other Native people, was very complicated. Unlike the societies found elsewhere in Canada, however, the Kwakwaka'wakw had a powerful nobility, which enjoyed both economic privileges, such as the right to have private property, and ritual ones, such as the right to sing certain songs and tell certain stories.

The Kwakwaka'wakw also had many elaborate rituals and ceremonies. The most famous of these is the potlatch, a word that derives from a Native word for "gift." A nobleman held a potlatch to celebrate special occasions such as a birth or marriage, or simply to show how wealthy he was. During the ceremony the host would hand out gifts to his guests, and elaborately dressed dancers performed stories that told the origins of the nobleman's wealth and privileges (*see* p. 96).

The Inuit people of the Arctic regions led a very different kind of life. The harsh environment and the scarcity of food meant that all food had to be shared. They also had to be on the move constantly to track down seals, walruses, and caribou. They traveled in a type of canoe known as an *umiak*, which could hold up to 20 people; on land they used a dog sled, called a *komatik*.

In the freezing winters, the Inuit lived in igloos, domed dwellings made out of blocks of ice, and in the summer, in tents made out of animal hide. In a society constantly threatened by mass starvation, nothing was wasted. Every part of the animal was either eaten, made into clothes and tools, or used for shelter.

**The word *Inuit*
means simply "the
people" and
covers many
cultural groups,
from the Yup'ik
people of Russian
Siberia to the
Inuit peoples of
Alaska, Canada,
and Greenland.**

THE FIRST EUROPEANS

The Norse, or Vikings, who were excellent seafarers, were probably the first Europeans to visit North America. The Vikings originally came from Norway, but by the tenth century, they had set up colonies on Iceland, a cold and treeless island far to the northwest of Europe, and on the southern coast of Greenland.

Scarcity of farmland drove the Vikings still farther westward. Their voyages to North America are recounted in two Icelandic sagas, or epic poems. Early in the 11th century, the sagas tell, Leif Eriksson landed on a fertile island that he called Vinland and founded a colony there. Some scholars believe that this was what is now Newfoundland. It seems probable that the Vikings also reached Nova Scotia.

In 1961 the Norwegian archaeologist Helge Ingstad discovered the remains of a Viking settlement at L'Anse aux Meadows on the northern tip of the island. Evidence suggests that the Vikings stayed for perhaps 15 years. The danger of the long, arduous voyages back to Norway and attacks from the natives probably forced the Vikings to abandon their American settlements.

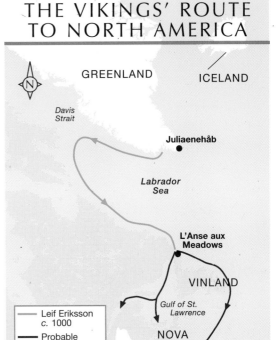

THE VIKINGS' ROUTE TO NORTH AMERICA

GREENLAND
ICELAND
Davis Strait
Juliaenehåb
Labrador Sea
L'Anse aux Meadows
VINLAND
Gulf of St. Lawrence
— Leif Eriksson c. 1000
— Probable Norse voyages
NOVA SCOTIA
Atlantic Ocean

The Vikings made their voyages in sturdy boats called longships. These measured between 45 and 75 feet (14 and 23 m) in length and carried a single square sail.

Icelandic sagas tell the story of Leif Eriksson's voyage to North America and his establishment of the colony of Vinland. Scholars debate exactly where this settlement was, but today the only archaeological evidence of the Vikings in North America is at L'Anse aux Meadows, on the northern coast of Newfoundland.

Like his contemporary Columbus, the Italian navigator John Cabot (Giovanni Caboto) dreamed of reaching Asia by sailing westward from Europe. On his second voyage to America in 1498, Cabot and his ships were lost at sea.

RIVAL COLONIES

Almost 500 years passed before Europeans returned to explore and settle North America once again. Toward the end of the 1400s, a race for riches began as explorers from France, England, Portugal, and Spain set off in search of fishing grounds, a northwest passage (sailing route) to Asia (*see* p. 56), and new lands and wealth to claim for their countries.

Cabot and Cartier

In 1497, just five years after the arrival of Columbus in America, the Italian-born navigator John Cabot (1450–1498) landed on Cape Breton Island. Although he found signs that the land was already inhabited, Cabot claimed the territory for the English king Henry VII, who had financed his voyage. He returned triumphantly to England, full of stories of a fertile land whose seas swarmed with fish. Indeed, it was Europe's fishermen who were the first to reap the rewards of Cabot's discovery.

It was not long before England's European neighbor, France, made a rival bid for the newly discovered territory. In 1534 the French king Francis I financed explorer Jacques Cartier (1491–1557) to sail to the Americas in the hope that he would discover new sources of riches. On his second trip to North America, Cartier sailed up the great St. Lawrence River, reaching as far as the island of Montréal. All the land he saw he claimed for France and called it New France. He also traded with the friendly Iroquois but eventually provoked hostilities by kidnapping one of their chiefs. After three separate trips to New France, Cartier returned to France with nothing more valuable than tall tales about rumored riches. Disappointed, the French lost interest in the Americas for more than half a century.

The Quest for Fur

Fur was the impetus for the next push to explore New France. At the beginning of the 17th century, fur was becoming fashionable in Europe, where the rich wore it as a trimming for their gowns and hats or as a winter lining. The wilderness of New France was reputed to be rich in beavers, otters, deer, foxes, and muskrats, whose pelts could more than meet the European demand for the costly luxury. The French king Henry IV saw an

Jacques Cartier is remembered in some of the street names of Québec's cities and towns. Montréal, whose site Cartier first discovered, has a famous square named in his honor—the lively and colorful Place Jacques-Cartier (*see* p. 39).

Cod Fishing off Newfoundland

LE GRAND BANC

Cod was only the first of Canada's abundant natural resources to attract significant numbers of Europeans to its shores. The waters off Newfoundland, known as the Grand Banks, swarmed with cod, and very soon after Cabot's discovery, many French and English fishermen sailed across the Atlantic to fish there. Once they had caught a full cargo of fish, the fishermen raced back to Europe to be the first to sell the season's catch—later in the season, prices fell sharply. After the discovery of the Grand Banks, cod—which could be salted and dried and thus kept for a long time—became an important and inexpensive part of the European diet. This early 18th-century French print shows ships and boats gathering on "Le Grand Banc" ("the grand bank").

The Northwest Passage

Many European explorers sought to find a sea passage around the near-frozen northern edge of the North American continent and thus a shorter route from Europe to the Far East. The venture was one of the great challenges of seafaring history.

John Cabot (*see* p. 54) made the first attempt in 1497 and ended up accidentally discovering Canada, though he got nowhere near the ice-packed Arctic Ocean. In 1611 the English explorer Henry Hudson followed the Canadian coast until he sailed into a vast, foggy sea. There he wandered aimlessly until he became caught in the harsh subarctic winter. His crew mutinied, casting Hudson, his son, and seven others adrift on a small boat. Neither Hudson nor his companions were ever heard from again, although what turned out to be the vast inland sea of Hudson Bay was named in his honor.

In the centuries that followed, a few daring explorers braved the fog, blizzards, and icebergs trying to find what was called the Northwest Passage. Many lost their lives in the attempt. It was only in 1906 that the first successful passage was made, by the Norwegian Roald Amundsen (1872–1928). This 19th-century illustration shows the ships *Erebus* and *Terror* as they wandered hopelessly through the gloomy, ice-packed sea.

In 1944 Canadian Henry Larsen (1899–1964) was the first to complete the journey in a single season. Larsen commanded a Royal Canadian Mounted Police ship that patrolled Canada's Arctic coast. Leaving Halifax, Nova Scotia, on July 22, the ship made the journey around the north of Canada and Alaska and arrived 86 days later in Vancouver, British Columbia. Larsen's vessel, the *St. Roch*, is proudly displayed at the Maritime Museum in Vancouver, British Columbia.

EARLY EUROPEAN SETTLEMENTS

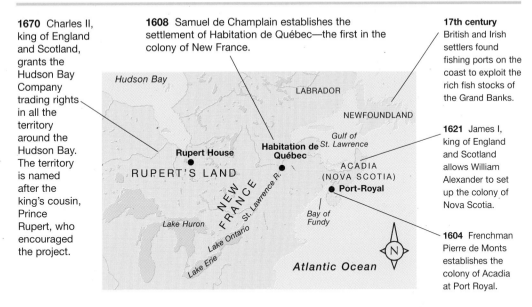

1670 Charles II, king of England and Scotland, grants the Hudson Bay Company trading rights in all the territory around the Hudson Bay. The territory is named after the king's cousin, Prince Rupert, who encouraged the project.

1608 Samuel de Champlain establishes the settlement of Habitation de Québec—the first in the colony of New France.

17th century British and Irish settlers found fishing ports on the coast to exploit the rich fish stocks of the Grand Banks.

1621 James I, king of England and Scotland allows William Alexander to set up the colony of Nova Scotia.

1604 Frenchman Pierre de Monts establishes the colony of Acadia at Port Royal.

opportunity to make some money out of the new French territory. He granted a fur-trading monopoly to a French aristocrat, Pierre du Gua, Sieur de Monts (c.1568–1630), on condition that de Monts found a permanent settlement in the territory.

In 1604 de Monts gathered a band of men and attempted to settle in the region around the Bay of Fundy, which they called Acadia. After several failed attempts, de Monts finally established the settlement of Port Royal on the coast of Nova Scotia. The settlement proved short-lived, however. De Monts and his men were too far removed from Canada's woodlands to enforce their trade monopoly properly. Poachers were able to take so many furs that the king eventually took away de Monts's trade monopoly and Port Royal was abandoned.

The Founding of Québec City
One member of de Monts's group was Samuel de Champlain (c.1567–1635). He was attracted to New France not only by the promise of profit, but also by the desire to establish a settlement "for the glory of God [and]

In the 17th century England and France competed to exploit the rich resources of the territory that later became Canada. At that time both Acadia and Nova Scotia covered roughly the area of Nova Scotia, Prince Edward Island, and New Brunswick.

Port Royal was later resettled and was Nova Scotia's capital until 1749. It also served as an important military base.

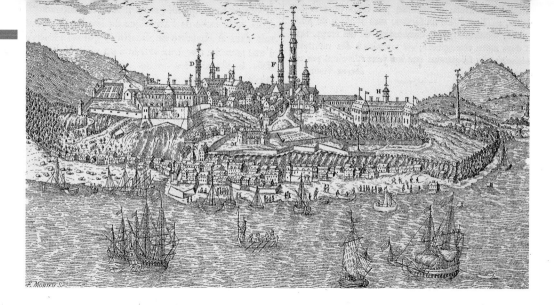

A 17th-century map shows the French cliff-top settlement of Habitation de Québec, overlooking the St. Lawrence River. At this time Québec City was the heart of the colony of New France. It was a busy port, handling the vast quantities of furs that were shipped back to France.

for the renown of the French." Champlain refused to give up the idea of establishing a colony, even after Port Royal was abandoned. He convinced the French king Henry IV to reinstate de Monts's trade monopoly for one more year, and in 1608 a second party of men made the journey to New France. They built a new settlement, this time on the banks of Canada's main waterway, the St. Lawrence River. The settlement, Habitation de Québec, eventually became Québec City, one of New France's most important forts (*see* pp. 20–21).

Champlain worked tirelessly to attract settlers to the colony. He spent years mapping the territory and helping to create trade routes for the French fur trade. Many historians believe that if Champlain had not persevered with his dream of a permanent settlement, the European presence in Canada would have disappeared in the early 17th century. For this reason Champlain is described as "the father of New France."

By 1663 Champlain's small, struggling colony was only a few hundred strong, and the colonists faced continual attacks from the Iroquois. France had a new king, Louis XIV, who was determined to see New France succeed. He declared it a royal colony and sent troops to defend it. To spur the colony's growth, the king sent over young women, called *filles du roi* ("daughters of the king"), and offered money to the colonists to marry them.

The French also set up the "seigneurial" system, under which huge tracts of land were granted to army officers, called *seigneurs*. The *seigneurs* divided their tracts into farms and attracted immigrant tenant farmers, called *habitants*. In exchange for the services of a gristmill and a priest, the tenants worked the land and paid taxes.

The Fur Trade Flourishes

By the end of the 1600s, the fur trade was booming and hundreds of Europeans who were eager to get rich came to New France. Traders arrived with goods such as knives, pots, and beads. At inland trading posts, they exchanged their wares for beaver pelts trapped by Native peoples. As the numbers of beavers in an area dropped, both traders and Native peoples moved farther across the continent in search of more animals. Conflicts arose when natives trespassed on the territory of other groups, and fighting also broke out between the French and the British. This struggle for control of the land and its fur trade continued throughout the 1700s.

As the fur trade moved farther across North America, *voyageurs* ("travelers") became the middlemen of the industry. They paddled canoes thousands of miles inland from Montréal to obtain furs from Native traders and returned several months later with their canoes full of pelts. These adventurous men explored and mapped many of North America's waterways.

Coureurs du Bois

The *coureurs du bois* ("wood-runners"), or *voyageurs* ("travelers"), were fur traders who traveled deep into the Canadian wilderness to trade with the Native populations, bartering inexpensive European goods, such as beads or pots and pans, for valuable beaver and otter pelts. Often the *coureurs* adopted Native dress, learned Native languages, and took Native wives. The children of these marriages usually became accepted members of their mothers' tribe and were called Métis (*see* p. 66) by the French. In today's Canada the Métis are recognized as a distinct Native group.

The Hudson's Bay Company still survives and is the oldest operating company in all of North America.

The series of wars fought between the French and British colonists in North America between 1689 and 1763 are known as the French and Indian Wars.

THE BRITISH CONQUEST OF CANADA

Until the late 1600s, the fur trade was mainly the domain of the merchants of the French settlement of Montréal. The fur trade changed dramatically in 1670, when a group of British merchants founded the Hudson's Bay Company. England's King Charles II granted the company a trading monopoly on all the land that had rivers draining into Hudson Bay. This area, Rupert's Land, covered more than three million square miles (8 million sq. km). Technically the land belonged to France, and conflicts arose between the English and French colonists.

In 1713 the British gained control of the French colony of Acadia. Later, as tensions increased between the two European powers, the British authorities deported Acadia's French-speaking farmers (*see* box opposite). The British and French rivalry reached a climax in 1756 with the outbreak of the Seven Years' War. This bitter war was fought in both Europe and America.

At first the French, fighting alongside their Native American allies, had the advantage on land and won a

French and British rivalry in America finally led to full-scale war in 1756. From 1758 the British conducted a campaign both on land and sea and were helped by their Native American allies. France finally surrendered in September 1763 and shortly after gave up its claims to the colonies of New France and Acadia.

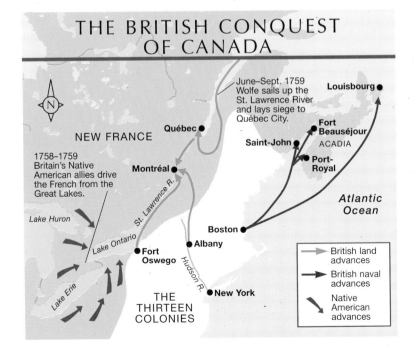

THE BRITISH CONQUEST OF CANADA

June–Sept. 1759 Wolfe sails up the St. Lawrence River and lays siege to Québec City.

Louisbourg

NEW FRANCE

Québec

Fort Beauséjour

ACADIA

Saint-John

1758–1759 Britain's Native American allies drive the French from the Great Lakes.

Montréal

Port-Royal

Atlantic Ocean

Lake Huron

St. Lawrence R.

Lake Ontario

Boston

Albany

Fort Oswego

Hudson R.

Lake Erie

THE THIRTEEN COLONIES

New York

British land advances

British naval advances

Native American advances

Acadia and the Acadians

The first French settlers of Canada inhabited an area that included present-day Nova Scotia, Prince Edward Island, and New Brunswick. They called the colony *Acadie* (Acadia). Some scholars say that Acadia got its name from the native Micmac word for "abundance," while others think that it was a corruption of Arcadia—the name of a Greek province that had long been a byword for a simple, country lifestyle.

Even after Champlain shifted the focus of French colonization to the more hospitable regions along the St. Lawrence River, the Acadians continued to prosper. The French and the British, meanwhile, constantly disputed ownership of the territory, and in 1713 Acadia finally became a British colony.

In 1754 the British governor, Charles Lawrence, demanded that the Acadians swear allegiance to the British king. The Acadians refused, and Lawrence set about forcibly expelling the Acadians from their traditional homeland.

Between 1755 and 1763, the British deported approximately 8,000 men, women, and children. The Acadians were often kept in temporary camps before deportation and many died of disease. Some crossed the Bay of Fundy to settle in New Brunswick and Maine. Others went north to Prince Edward Island or to the two barren islands of St. Pierre and Miquelon, off the southern

coast of Newfoundland. Still others went all the way to Louisiana, where the name "Acadian " became "Cajun" and the people became the basis for another transplanted French culture.

In the 19th century, American poet Henry Wadsworth Longfellow wrote the poem "Evangeline," whose imaginary heroine lives in Acadia with her father at the time of the expulsion. This statue of Evangeline stands in St. Martinville, Louisiana, where many Acadians settled.

string of victories. In 1758 the tide turned as the British exploited their naval superiority. British ships raided the coast of Acadia (Nova Scotia) and Cape Breton Island, both of which were again in French hands. The fall of the French fort of Louisbourg on Cape Breton Island and other forts in Acadia enabled the British to sail up the St. Lawrence River and to launch an assault on Québec City. On September 13, 1759, the two sides fought the decisive Battle of the Plains of Abraham.

In this battle the British commander Major-General James Wolfe (1727–1759) led 3,000 soldiers in a surprise attack against the French forces of the Marquis de Montcalm (1712–1759). The two armies met on the Plains of Abraham, which lay beneath Québec's landward defenses. In just 15 minutes, the British won the fight and took possession of Québec City. Both Wolfe and the Marquis de Montcalm were fatally wounded in the assault. In 1760 Montréal, too, fell into British hands, and with it dominion over Canada.

In Europe the war between France and Britain continued until 1763, when France finally signed the Treaty

The loss of New France famously provoked the French king's mistress Madame de Pompadour to declare: "It makes little difference—Canada is useful only to provide me with furs."

The Siege of Québec, 1759

The British besieged Québec City for months before winning the Battle of the Plains of Abraham. Marie de la Visitation, a French nun at the General Hospital of Québec, survived the siege, and later described it in a letter:

The only rest we partook of, was during prayers, and still it was not without interruption from the noise of shells and shot, dreading every moment that they would be directed toward us. The red-hot shot and carcasses terrified those who attended the sick during the night. They had the affliction of witnessing the destruction of the houses of the citizens…we could offer nothing but our tears and prayers…We witnessed the carnage from our windows…We were in the midst of the dead and dying, who were brought in by the hundreds, many of them our close connexions [friends and relatives]; it was necessary to smother our griefs and exert ourselves to relieve them.

of Paris and officially gave New France and Acadia to Britain. The French North American empire was effectively at an end, although France kept Louisiana until 1803. The British conquest of Canada was to have far-reaching consequences. It gave Britain a useful base during the American Revolution (1776–1783) and provided a rich supply of timber to help build Britain's growing global empire.

THE BRITISH IN CHARGE

The British now faced the difficult problem of how to deal with their new French subjects, the Canadiens. The initial British plan was to fill the colony with English-speaking Protestants. To attract the new immigrants, they changed the colony's name to Québec, abolished the seigneurial system, and took away the political rights of the Roman Catholic Canadiens.

In 1774 a new law attempted to improve relations with the unhappy Canadiens. The Quebec Act of 1774 gave Catholics back their full rights and re-established the seigneurial system. The British attempt to reconcile the Canadiens paid off during the American Revolution. While the Canadiens refused to fight with the British against the American rebels, they also declined to join the latter in their struggle.

The final victory of the American revolutionaries in 1783 sped up the development of Britain's remaining North American colonies. Some 40,000 American colonists who had remained loyal to Britain during the war moved north to the British-run territories. Most settled in Nova Scotia and New Brunswick, but about 8,000 went to the western part of Québec, where they settled the area that later became the province of Ontario.

In 1770 American artist Benjamin West movingly depicted the death of Major-General Wolfe at the Battle of the Plains of Abraham in 1759. Wolfe is shown dying surrounded by his officers and allies, including a Native American chief. The original painting hangs in the National Gallery in Ottawa, Ontario; this rendition is one of the many copies made of this famous painting.

THE CONSTITUTIONAL ACT

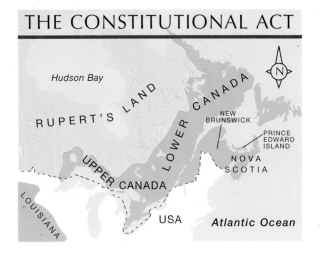

Hudson Bay

RUPERT'S LAND

UPPER CANADA

LOUISIANA

LOWER CANADA

NEW BRUNSWICK

PRINCE EDWARD ISLAND

NOVA SCOTIA

USA

Atlantic Ocean

N

The Constitutional Act of 1791 divided the old French colony into Upper Canada and Lower Canada. Rupert's Land remained in the hands of the Hudson's Bay Company until 1870, when it was sold to Canada.

The Two Canadas

Having lost the Thirteen Colonies, Britain was eager to keep everyone in its remaining North American colonies happy. The colonies of Nova Scotia, New Brunswick, and Prince Edward Island presented few problems, as most people living in these areas were of British descent. In Québec, however, there was an uneasy mix of French and English colonists. In 1791 Britain passed the Constitutional Act in an attempt to please both colonial groups.

The act split Québec into two—Upper and Lower Canada. British-dominated Upper Canada was modeled after the British colonial system, while the French-dominated Lower Canada was allowed to keep its seigneurial system and Roman Catholic religion. Both provinces were given an elected assembly, although real power lay in the hands of governors appointed by Britain.

The War of 1812

Increasing numbers of new settlers came to British North America, and between 1783 and 1812, the population of the colonies tripled. Nevertheless, tensions between Britain and the United States still deterred many potential settlers.

On June 18, 1812, the United States declared war on Britain and launched an attack on Canada. The U.S. army seized control of Lake Erie and some of Upper Canada. In response Britain imposed a naval blockade on America's Atlantic seaboard, and in 1814 a British raiding force was able to march on Washington and set fire to many government buildings. The war reached a stalemate, and the United States finally formally recognized the British colonies and a border was fixed.

THE BIRTH OF A NATION

After 1814 the Canadian colonies flourished. Despite the growing prosperity, however, colonists in both Upper and Lower Canada grew increasingly unhappy with their governments. Finally in 1837 revolts broke out in both colonies, and although they were suppressed, the British government was worried enough to make some changes.

Under the Act of Union of 1840, Upper and Lower Canada were united, with a single assembly and governor. The union of the two Canadas, the British believed, would stimulate the economy of the whole St. Lawrence Valley area and enable the colony to compete with its energetic neighbor to the south, the United States. They also hoped that union would help to reconcile the French to British colonial rule.

The Growth of Self-rule

Gradually each of the colonies was able to develop self-rule, setting up laws and institutions that were

CONFEDERATION

In the 1860s Canada was still a loose collection of separate colonies. In 1867, under the terms of the British North America Act, the colonies were able to join the new Dominion of Canada. Eventually all the old colonies voted to join the confederation. Meanwhile, as new lands were settled in the Canadian West, new provinces were also created as part of the Dominion.

NEWFOUNDLAND
1949

PRINCE
EDWARD
ISLAND
1873

BRITISH
COLUMBIA
1871   ALBERTA
1905

MANITOBA
1870

QUÉBEC
1867

ONTARIO
1867

NOVA
SCOTIA
1867

OTTAWA ●

NEW BRUNSWICK
1867

SASKATCHEWAN
1905

The far west of Canada was first explored at the end of the 18th century. In 1793 Alexander Mackenzie became the first European to cross North America north of Mexico. The river that flows northwest from Great Slave Lake to the Beaufort Sea bears his name.

independent of the British administration. The colonies, however, also remained independent of each other. On the eastern seaboard, Newfoundland lived off its fisheries, Prince Edward Island was a prosperous farming community, while New Brunswick and Nova Scotia had flourishing shipbuilding industries. On the Pacific coast was the recently settled colony of British Columbia.

In between were Rupert's Land, administered by the Hudson's Bay Company and the North-Western Territory, both home to numerous Native peoples. Only the Red River Colony, based on an area around the present-day Winnipeg, was settled. Here lived a community of Métis—people of combined French and Native ancestry—and a small number of white British settlers.

The leaders of the eastern colonies soon recognized the benefits that would come from a united colony. They would be able not only to improve trade and provide for better defense against possible aggression from the United States but also to manage the westward expansion of Canada.

The Red River Rebellion

The 5,000 or so Métis who lived in the Red River Colony were particularly resentful of Canada's attempts to push its territory westward. The new dominion bought the Red River Colony's land from the Hudson's Bay Company, and government surveyors set about dividing the land into lots, all without consulting the people who lived there.

To challenge Canada's expansion, in 1869 Louis Riel (1844–1885) led the Métis in setting up their own government at Fort Garry. In an effort to bring about a peaceful solution to the crisis, the Ottawa parliament passed the Manitoba Act, which set up the new province of Manitoba, to be run by the Métis, and gave a pardon to the rebels.

The few British settlers in the area, however, refused to accept Ottawa's decision. The Canadian government now decided to send in soldiers to the area to restore order, and Riel went into exile in the United States.

Many of the Métis moved westward into the territory that later became the province of Saskatchewan. In 1885 Riel led the Métis in another rebellion; this time he was captured and executed by the federal government.

In 1864 representatives of the colonies met in Québec City to discuss the possibility of forming a single nation—a process known as confederation. It was not until 1866, however, that representatives from the Canadas, New Brunswick, and Nova Scotia finally met in London, England, to draw up an agreement called the British North America Act. On July 1, 1867, the British parliament passed the act and the four colonies were united as "one Dominion under the name of Canada." The capital of the new nation was Ottawa, chosen by Queen Victoria.

Westward Expansion

The new Dominion of Canada was led by Prime Minister John A. Macdonald (1815–1891). He dreamed of a country that stretched from the Atlantic to the Pacific. In time his dream came true, as each of the colonies joined the confederation. The central Canadian colony of Manitoba joined in 1870, despite its inhabitants' initial reluctance. British Columbia, which had been settled by immigrants only a few years before, joined in 1871. Prince Edward Island joined Canada in 1873, while Alberta and Saskatchewan joined in 1905. Newfoundland was the last province to join the confederation, choosing to remain a colony until 1949.

When the Canadian West joined the confederation in the late 1800s, there were very few established settlements. To strengthen the area against an American invasion, the Canadian government tried attracting settlers to the area by advertising vast tracts of inexpensive, fertile farmland. Between 1897 and 1911, more than two million people flooded into the Canadian West from the United States and Europe. This great western push,

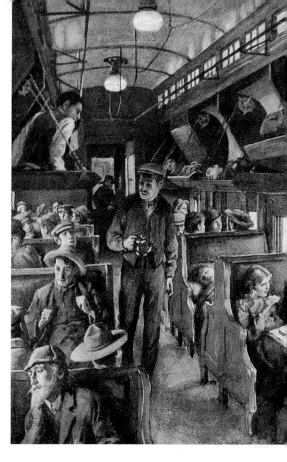

In 1886 the first train ran from Montréal to Vancouver, and immigrants swarmed into Alberta and Saskatchewan in search of farmlands and a new life. Immigration to Canada reached its peak in 1913, when more than 400,000 people arrived.

The Great Klondike Gold Rush

The Klondike is a small, icy stream that flows from the Ogilvie Mountains in northern Canada down into the great Yukon River. It was along the banks of the Klondike River in 1896 that pioneer Robert Henderson discovered gold, sparking the Great Klondike Gold Rush.

Returning down the Klondike, Henderson met with another gold-hunter, George Washington Carmack, and his two Native friends, Skookum Jim and Dawson Charley. Henderson told Carmack about his discovery and famously told him that Native peoples were not welcome there. Carmack and his friends got angry with Henderson and went off to prospect a different area. On August 15, Skookum Jim struck lucky, panning $4 worth of gold in Bonanza Creek, and the following day, the three friends rushed off to register their find. Meanwhile Henderson, searching just a few miles away, found almost nothing.

Within months, thousands of people were trekking to the Yukon in the hope of striking it rich. The map below shows the major routes that people took to reach the creek. Of the routes the easiest and most expensive was the 1,300-mile (2,090 km) journey by steamer up the Yukon River (shown in green). Other routes were more hazardous. Many hiked from the southern Alaskan ports of Skagway and Dyea (purple), while a few struggled through the Canadian wilderness from Edmonton (red). Of the 750 or so who braved this last route, only 160 made it to Dawson, the gold-rush town that sprang up near the Klondike. Historians estimate that, all in all, more than one million people left their homes and headed for the Yukon. Only a handful made their fortune from the trip; most gave up on the way. Both successful and unsuccessful prospectors, however, helped to settle and develop British Columbia.

St. Michael
Beaufort Sea
Yukon R.
ALASKA (TERRITORY OF THE U.S.)
NORTHWEST TERRITORIES
Dawson
Klondike R.
YUKON
Whitehorse
Dyea
Skagway
N
Pacific Ocean
ALBERTA
BRITISH COLUMBIA
Edmonton

spurred by the newly completed Trans-Canada Railroad (*see* p. 92), was the last great migration in North American history.

An Emerging Power

Before the 20th century, Canada lacked a strong identity. Many people saw it simply as part of the British empire. World War I (1914–1918) played an important role in shaping a Canadian identity and also strengthened the nation's industry and its international reputation.

Some 625,000 Canadians served in the war, fighting in some of its most important battles. In 1917 all four divisions of Canadian soldiers fought together for the first time at the Battle of Vimy Ridge, in northern France. Their bravery and efficiency in this battle earned Canada the respect of its allies, although the cost was high.

Back at home the war forced Canada to develop new industries rapidly to supply the war effort with huge amounts of metals, grain, livestock, and wood in addition to manufactured goods such as munitions, airplanes, and ships. By the war's end, Canada had become the world's seventh-largest industrial nation.

Canada's achievements in the war won it the gratitude and respect of all its allies, but particularly of Britain, for which it was still nominally a dominion. In 1931 the British parliament passed an act—the Statute of Westminster—that gave Canada and other British dominions full independence.

From the Great Depression to World War II

In the decade following World War I, Canada flourished until the collapse of the U.S. stock market in the Wall Street Crash of 1929. Almost overnight thousands of Canadians lost their money. In the Great Depression that followed, one in four Canadians lost their jobs. The farmers of the Prairie provinces were particularly hard hit. Their wheat became almost worthless, and in the early 1930s, a severe drought made their situation even worse.

During World War I, almost 60,000 Canadian soldiers were killed in action. Another 173,000 were injured.

The Statute of Westminster (1931) also created the British Commonwealth, of which Canada became a member. The Commonwealth is a group of Britain's former dominions and colonies that continue to recognize the British crown as their sovereign.

To counteract the effects of the Great Depression, the Canadian government experimented with new social programs, laying down the first foundations of a national welfare system. A new trade treaty with the United States in 1936 helped stimulate Canada's industry.

When World War II broke out in 1939, Canada again supported Britain. By the war's end, almost a million Canadians had gone overseas. Canadians served in places as far away as Hong Kong, and in 1944 the Canadian army was assigned one of the Normandy beaches to attack in the D-Day landings in France.

At home the Great Depression ended and the economy boomed as Canada's industries produced the huge amounts of raw materials—even the uranium ore that produced the world's first atomic bombs—food, and machinery that were needed for the Allied war effort. By the end of the war, Canada's industry had grown to become the fourth largest in the world. The government had also extended the welfare system, introducing benefits to support families, and a massive housing program.

During the Great Depression, the Canadian government discouraged immigration. After World War II, however, Canada welcomed refugees from all over the world.

CANADA TODAY

Since the end of World War II in 1945, Canada has continued to distinguish itself in the world, while striving to keep its people united. The country has faced many challenges from within as Canadians have fought for social change. Among those groups that have brought about the most dramatic changes in Canadian society are the Native peoples and the French Canadians.

Native Lands, Native Rights

When Native peoples encountered Europeans over 500 years ago, they were faced with many devastating changes, including the introduction of firearms, alcohol, and unfamiliar diseases such as typhoid, smallpox, and measles to which they had no immunity. Within two centuries of the Europeans' arrival, the Native population of Canada fell by as much as 95 percent.

Those who survived often lost their traditional way of life. The French and British authorities forced them off their land, kept them almost as prisoners on small areas of land called reserves, and limited their political rights. In 1857 the Upper and Lower Canada colonies even passed an act to "Encourage the Gradual Civilization of the Indian [Native] Tribes." Under the act a committee of white men could vote a "well-behaved" Native to become "white." Some people argue that many of the past policies of the Canadian government were genocidal; that is, they aimed to wipe out the Native peoples and their cultures.

Many Native peoples fought as soldiers in the world wars, and it became increasingly difficult for the government to ignore their claims to land and equal rights. The 1951 Indian Act began to make some concessions, but it was only in 1960, however, that the Native populations won the right to vote in federal elections.

It took even longer for the Canadian government to recognize Native land rights. From the 1970s Native groups, such as the powerful Assembly of First Nations (AFN), began to contest land ownership through the courts; occasionally some tribes used violent protest. They

The first reserve of land set aside for Native peoples was at Sillery in New France in 1637.

The Native peoples of Canada highly value the land and its resources. Below is a typical Inuit settlement, which lies in the Inuit homeland of Nunavut.

This is the flag for Nunavut. The blue and gold represent the richness of the landscape. The red and blue symbolize the union with Canada. The stone in the middle is an inuksuk, an Inuit monument found throughout the Arctic. The star is the North Star.

often based their legal arguments on the Royal Proclamation of 1763, which had affirmed the right of the First Peoples not to be "disturbed or molested" on their lands, but which governments had ignored.

In May 1993 the Inuit people of the Canadian Arctic won a brilliant victory. Under the Land Claim Agreement of that year, the federal government agreed to hand over some 136,500 square miles (350,000 sq. km) of land to the Inuit people—the biggest Native land claim settlement in Canadian history. The government also agreed to the formation of a new territory, Nunavut (*see* box opposite).

Such mass transfers of land are helping to lessen the prejudices Native peoples have faced under the past policies of the Canadian government. Native peoples hope to ease their peoples' hardships by starting new businesses and sharing in the profits from the harvest of natural resources. They also hope to control the exploitation of their lands by non-Natives. In the meantime most Native peoples, both on reserves and in Canadian cities, continue to endure prejudice as well as lower standards of living than those enjoyed by other Canadians.

"Maîtres chez nous"

Canadians call the time when Britain took over New France "the Conquest" (*see* p. 60). From then until the mid-20th century, English was the language of business, government, and commerce in Québec, even though the majority of people living there spoke French. It was difficult for francophones to hold important jobs. Many French-speaking people worried that, unless something was done, their language and culture would disappear.

After World War II, French speakers embraced a new political idea that was summed up in the slogan "*Maîtres chez nous*" ("masters of our own house"). In 1960 Québec's government introduced a series of laws to protect the French language and culture. These laws had such an influence on the province that they are known

Québec is economically powerful—it is the fourth-largest producer of electricity in the world, and its forests produce one-fifth of the world's pulp and paper.

Nunavut—"Our Land"

Early in 1999 the Inuit celebrated the establishment of the Territory of Nunavut. Nunavut means "our land," and the Inuit are the first Native people of North America to gain self-government. On July 9 every year, the Inuit celebrate Nunavut Day—the anniversary of the day in 1993 when the federal government and the Inuit people signed the Land Claim Agreement, which set up the new territory.

Nunavut, a huge chunk of land carved out of the old Northwest Territories, covers some 136,500 square miles (350,000 sq. km) in the eastern Arctic, amounting to one-fifth of Canada's territory. It stretches from the tip of Ellesmere Island—just 248 miles (400 km) from the North Pole—to the wind-swept Belcher Islands, deep in Hudson Bay.

Despite Nunavut's vast size, it has a tiny population—just 22,000—17,500 of whom are Inuit. There are no roads to the territory from the rest of Canada. Its settlements are often hundreds of miles from each other and are connected only by internal flights. The capital, Iqaluit, on Baffin Island, lies 1,250 miles (2,000 km) north of Ottawa, Ontario.

Nunavut remains part of the Canadian confederation, but by 2009 an elected Inuit government will have assumed all the responsibilities once exercised by the government of the Northwest Territories.

These responsibilities include the administration of such areas as public housing, culture, and health care.

Nunavut's chief treasures are its vast natural resources and the beauty of its lonely landscapes. The Nunavut government shares responsibility with Ottawa for the management of the territory's environment and has a share in the federal government's royalties from oil, gas, and mineral development on nationally owned lands.

There are plans to set up three more federally funded national parks in Nunavut, and the Inuit people are developing the territory's rich potential as a major tourist destination.

The Official Languages Act

In 1969, in an attempt to lessen the tensions between French- and English-speaking Canada, the federal government passed a law that made English and French the two official languages of Canada. Both now have equal status in the governments and courts. The law was not easily accepted by some English speakers, and there is still some resentment over official bilingualism and biculturalism.

as the Quiet Revolution. At this time French speakers in Québec also rejected the term "French Canadian" in favor of the French word *Québécois*, ("inhabitant of Québec").

By the end of the 1960s, Québec's sense of pride in its culture had grown. A politician named René Levesque helped form a new political party, whose main aim was to see Québec become an independent nation. The party, called the Parti Québécois, was elected to lead the province in 1976 and has held power on and off in Québec ever since.

In 1980 a Parti Québécois government held a referendum on the issue of Québec sovereignty. Sixty percent of the people of Québec voted against separating from Canada. This was because anglophones, Native peoples, and many francophones believed that they would lose out if Québec became independent.

When the federal government added the Charter of Rights and Freedoms to the constitution in 1982, many Québécois were not happy with the changes. Their provincial government wanted the document changed to

These Québécois are rallying for an independent Québec. The blue flag decorated with four fleur-de-lys, or lilies, is Québec's flag and a symbol of Québécois nationalism (see pp. 8 and 119)

recognize Québec's unique culture and to grant it many of the federal government's powers. These demands were hotly debated all over the country, and Canada's leaders made two major attempts to reach a constitutional compromise with Québec: the Meech Lake Accord (1987) and the Charlottetown Accord (1992). Both attempts failed to win support as many Canadians objected to giving Québec a special status.

The Québecois were disappointed over the failure of the accords and elected a powerful new separatist party, the Bloc Québécois, to sit in Canada's federal parliament. They also reelected the Parti Québécois to control their provincial government.

In 1995 the Parti Québécois called a second referendum on Québec's separation from Canada. Unlike the 1980 referendum, in which a clear majority voted to remain in Canada, in the second referendum 49.4 percent of Québecois voted to separate. Canadians were shocked and alarmed at how close their country had come to breaking up. Québec separatists, bitterly disappointed by their narrow loss, vowed to continue fighting.

GOVERNMENT IN CANADA

Canada's democratic government is committed to balancing the interests of Canadians as a whole with the individual freedom of its citizens. Canadians are able to practice different lifestyles and religions and express their beliefs and points of view without fear of legal penalties.

In 1996 the former Bloc Québécois leader Lucien Bouchard became leader of the provincial Parti Québécois and the premier of Québec. He is committed to an independent Québec.

The October Crisis

In October 1970 Canada was rocked by crisis. A radical separatist group known as the Front de Libération du Québec (FLQ) kidnapped two government officials, including the province's minister of labor, Pierre Laporte. In exchange for the release of their hostages, the group demanded publicity for its cause, which was Québec's political freedom.

The prime minister, Pierre Trudeau, refused to give in to the FLQ's terrorist tactics, and parliament passed the War Measures Act. This act imposed martial (wartime) law and allowed the police to arrest anyone suspected of having connections with the FLQ. The next night Laporte was found murdered. The other hostage was eventually freed. Although the vast majority of Québecois condemned the FLQ's use of violence, this "October Crisis," as it was called, did not lessen support for separatism.

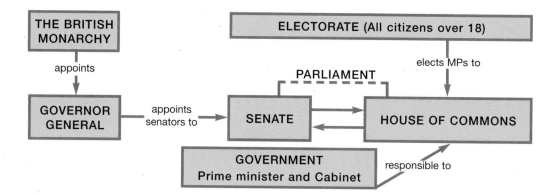

THE BRITISH MONARCHY

appoints

GOVERNOR GENERAL

appoints senators to

ELECTORATE (All citizens over 18)

elects MPs to

PARLIAMENT

SENATE

HOUSE OF COMMONS

GOVERNMENT
Prime minister and Cabinet

responsible to

This chart shows how Canada is governed. The British monarch has no real power—the Crown's representative, the governor general, acts only on the advice of the prime minister.

The government operates on three levels: federal, provincial or territorial, and municipal. The federal government is in charge of affairs that affect the entire country, such as national defense, international trade, banking, criminal law, and the monetary system.

The ten provincial and three territorial governments handle regional issues such as education, property rights, law courts, natural resources, and hospitals. Canada has close to 5,000 municipal governments based in its cities, towns, and counties. They control the city police, fire-fighting services, roads, libraries, and other local responsibilities. Each level of government collects taxes.

The Canadian Constitution

In 1982 the Canadian government brought home the country's constitution, which had been kept in Britain since 1867. Until it was brought to Canada, the constitution had been known as the British North America Act. After its repatriation it was called the Constitution Act. The constitution describes in writing Canada's system of government, laws, and courts. It describes which powers belong to the federal and provincial governments, and affirms the treaties with and rights of Canada's First Nations and Inuit peoples.

The Charter of Rights and Freedoms was added to the constitution in 1982. It protects Canadians' basic rights, such as the rights to self-expression, worship, vote, and freedom from discrimination.

The British monarch is the head of state and is represented on a day-to-day basis by the governor general, whom the monarch appoints on the prime minister's recommendation. The governor general performs many duties, including appointing new senators, officially recognizing a new prime minister and members of the House of Commons, and giving Royal Assent to bills, which then become laws.

The upper house, called the Senate (*Sénat*), is an unelected assembly whose members, called senators, are appointed by the governor general on the advice of the prime minister. The Senate reviews and votes on a bill after it has been passed by the House of Commons. Senators also propose and pass new bills that do not involve spending or collecting tax dollars. Senators can hold office until they reach 75 years of age.

The House of Commons (*Chambre des communes*) is an assembly led by the prime minister. Its 301 members, called members of parliament (MPs), are elected by the public. The House of Commons is where most of Canada's laws and political decisions are made. Each day in the House, MPs discuss laws and current events, make speeches, and vote on bills. MPs belong to different political parties.

The prime minister is the leader of the party with the most members in the House of Commons, and he or she makes important day-to-day decisions about the welfare of Canadians. The prime minister is aided by a Cabinet of about 30 ministers, who are selected from

All Canadian women and men 18 years of age and older have the right to vote in elections. Elections are by secret ballot and are held every four to five years.

The Canadian Senate and House of Commons are both located in the parliament buildings in Ottawa, Ontario.

Recent prime
ministers of
Canada have
been:

**Recent prime
ministers of
Canada have
been:**

- **Pierre Trudeau
  (1968–1979
  and 1980–1984)**
- **Charles
  Joseph Clark
  (1979–1980)**
- **John Napier
  Turner (1984)**
- **Brian Mulroney
  (1984–1993)**
- **A. Kim Campbell
  (1993)—
  Canada's first
  woman prime
  minister**
- **Jean Chrétien
  (1993–)**

the House and sometimes from other public bodies, such as the universities. Each minister leads a different department of the government, such as finance or defense. Opposition parties are those that have fewer members in the House of Commons than the governing party. They suggest changes to bills and keep track of the government.

The focus of the workday in the House of Commons is Question Period, which lasts 45 minutes. During this time members of the opposition challenge the prime minister and Cabinet members face to face, posing questions, making speeches, and sometimes hurling accusations.

Political Parties and Elections

Although there are many different political parties in Canada, only a few are widely popular, and only two, the Liberals and Progressive Conservatives, have ever governed federally. The Liberal Party promotes a middle ground between socialist programs and business interests. The Progressive Conservative Party has competed with the Liberals since confederation and promotes the interests of business.

THE CANADIAN PARLIAMENT TODAY

Prime Minister Jean Chrétien

House of Commons/ Chambre des Communes
301 members • Last election 1997 • Elections held every 4–5 years

LP Liberal Party	52%
RP Reform Party	19%
BQ Bloc Québécois	14%
NDP New Democratic Party	7%
PCP Progressive Conservative Party	7%
Independents	1%

Senate/Sénat
105 members • No elections—senators are nominated on a provincial basis

LP Liberal party	51%
PCP Progressive Conservative Party	40%
Others and independents	9%

Elections were held in Canada in 1997. The Liberal Party continued to increase in popularity, and Jean Chrétien was elected to a second term of office as prime minister.

The Mounties

The Canadian Mountie, dressed in a distinctive red uniform and broad-brimmed hat, is one of Canada's most famous national symbols. The Royal Canadian Mounted Police (RCMP), nicknamed the Mounties, was originally called the North West Mounted Police. The force was created in 1873 to keep order in the vast North-West Territories.

The new force proved its worth during the Great Klondike Gold Rush (*see* p. 68). Superintendent Sam Steele and his men kept the peace, confiscated handguns, controlled gambling, and turned away troublemakers. Sam Steele has since become a Canadian legend, helping to create the clean-cut, determined image associated with the Mounties. Relations between the Mounties and Native peoples, however, have often been difficult. Today the RCMP is a national force that provides policing in all Canada's provinces and territories, except Québec and Ontario.

The New Democratic Party (NDP) was created in the 1960s to represent organized labor and campaigns to expand Canada's social programs. The Reform Party, formed in the 1980s, is based in Canada's western provinces. It urges financial restraint and a "no compromise" approach to Québec's constitutional demands. Since the early 1990s, the Bloc Québécois has represented the cause of Québec independence in Canada's parliament.

In a national election, all 301 seats in the House of Commons become available. Candidates from different political parties compete for each seat, and whoever gets the most votes wins the seat and becomes an MP. The party that wins the most seats governs the country.

Provincial elections are similar to national ones. Each province has a legislative assembly, which is elected by the people. The head of the provincial government is called the premier, and he or she appoints a Cabinet.

The Economy

"Throughout history trade has been critical to Canada's livelihood... Few countries in the world are so dependent on trade."

Twentieth-century Canadian prime minister Brian Mulroney

Canadians are fortunate to live in one of the wealthiest countries in the world. Canada is a member of the Group of 8 (G-8), the eight countries of the world with the most powerful economies. The other members of the G-8 are the United States, Britain, France, Germany, Italy, Japan, and Russia.

Canada has a strong economy for a number of reasons. Most importantly this vast, sparsely populated country has far more valuable natural resources—oil, uranium, wood, and hydroelectricity among them—and agricultural goods than Canadians need. These large surpluses are exported, or sold, to other countries. Because they earn so much money on exports, Canadians can also afford to import, or bring in, thousands of different products. Canadians themselves are a valuable part of their economy; they make up one of the most highly skilled and educated workforces in the world.

MAIN ECONOMIC SECTORS	THE WORKFORCE
as % of GNP	%
66.9 Services	73 Services
30.5 Industry	23 Industry
2.6 Agriculture	4 Agriculture
Source: Government of Canada, 1996	Source: Government of Canada, 1996

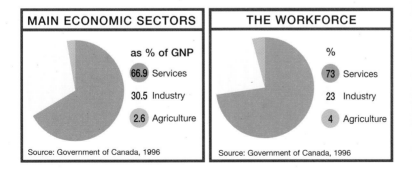

A boom boat gathers together floating logs for a sawmill on west Vancouver Island. Canada is the world's largest exporter of forest products.

In 1996 Canada enjoyed a large trading surplus (the value of its exports minus the value of its imports)— some 30 billion U.S. dollars.

Canada exports much more than it imports. Its chief exports arise from its wealth of natural resources, including lumber and oil and gas.

TRADING PARTNERS

Canada's history has always been closely tied to its trade. The Native communities were enthusiastic traders, and the British and French first colonized the country in order to exploit its rich supply of cod and fur.

Today Canada is the ninth-biggest trading nation in the world, accounting for some 3.5 percent of total world exports. The amount of trade between Canada and the United States is the highest in the world between any two nations. About 80 percent of Canadian products are exported to the United States, and Canada imports more American goods than any other country.

Until the early 1980s, Great Britain was Canada's second-largest trade partner, but since then Canada has traded more with Japan and other Pacific Rim countries.

The Free Trade Agreement

In 1989 Canada and the United States entered into the Free Trade Agreement (FTA), which allows goods to cross the border between the countries without any tariffs or duties being added to their price. The agreement also removed penalties against companies leaving Canada to produce their goods in the United States. The North American Free Trade Agreement (NAFTA) came into effect in 1994. It reduces restrictions on goods and services traded between Canada, the United States, and Mexico. Canadian workers complain that NAFTA has forced them to accept U.S. working practices, which offer less favorable working conditions than those traditionally enjoyed in Canada.

Although more than 80 percent of goods crossing the Canada–U.S. border were duty-free before the

EXPORTS ($bn)	
● Vehicles and transport	46.6
● Industrial machinery	45.7
● Industrial supplies	38.3
● Forest products	25.4
● Energy products	18.8
● Agricultural goods	17.9
Total (inc. Others)	205.8

IMPORTS ($bn)	
● Industrial machinery	56.3
● Vehicles and transport	37.8
● Industrial supplies	34.2
● Consumer goods	19.0
● Agricultural goods	10.4
● Energy products	7.1
Total (inc. Others)	175.7

Source: Government of Canada, 1996

FTA was signed, many Canadians also feel that the agreement has harmed their economy. Many people believe the agreement gives the United States and Mexico an unfair advantage because goods are cheaper to produce in those countries than in Canada. Canadian-made products often cannot compete. Since the FTA came into effect, thousands of manufacturing jobs have disappeared in Canada.

MAIN ECONOMIC SECTORS

Canada's principal wealth lies in its natural resources—in the great, dark forests that cover the northern reaches of the provinces, in the vast, fertile prairielands, and in the mineral-rich territories of the far north.

MAIN TRADING PARTNERS

EXPORTS	IMPORTS

%		%	
79.1	USA	75.9	USA
4.5	Japan	3.0	Japan
1.7	United Kingdom	2.3	United Kingdom
14.7	Other	18.8	Other

Source: Government of Canada

Canada's trade is overwhelmingly with its neighbor, the United States. Under the North American Free Trade Agreement (NAFTA), Canada can export its goods freely into the United States and Mexico. On the other hand, under the same agreement, Canada has to import the cheaper goods produced in these countries.

Canada's "Green Gold"

Trees cover almost half of Canada, so it is not surprising that this huge country is the world's largest exporter of forest products, including lumber, plywood, shingles, rayon, newsprint, and paper. Forests are also important tourist attractions that provide jobs for rangers and guides, among others. They provide Canadians with their largest industry and are often referred to as "green gold."

Most of the forests in Canada are owned and managed by the government on behalf of all Canadians. Logging companies must obtain permission to cut down trees. They must also take measures to protect young trees, old trees, and the rich wildlife that depends on them. There have been many conflicts between logging companies on the one hand, and environmentalists and Native groups on the other. One well-known area of conflict is Temagami in northern Ontario. Logging companies want to harvest the old-growth forests there, but environmental groups want this unique habitat to be protected.

Agriculture: Four Regions

Canada is a world-leading food producer. Agriculture and food industries form the nation's third-largest source of employment. Since 1900, however, the number of farms has decreased from about 700,000 to fewer than 300,000. This does not mean people are in danger of going hungry. On average, farms today are almost four times larger than farms in the past, and farmers can produce ten times more thanks to machinery, pesticides, and healthier, stronger, faster-growing seeds and plants.

*This map shows
how Canadian
territory
divides between
various uses.*

LAND USE

Tundra

Cropland

Forest

Pasture

High mountains

Only about 7 percent of Canada's land is suitable for farming, but this small percentage equals 231,107 square miles (598,567 sq. km) of land—an area slightly smaller than the size of Texas. Most farms are located in southern areas within 300 miles (500 km) of the U.S. border, where the climate is mildest, the land most fertile, and crops can be quickly transported to markets in the United States before spoiling.

Canada has four main agricultural regions distinguished according to type of soil, plants, and weather conditions. These are called the Atlantic, Central, Prairie, and Pacific regions, and each is suitable for different types of farming. In the Pacific region, cattle ranching is popular, as is fruit and vegetable farming. The Prairie region has about 75 percent of Canada's farmland and specializes in grain crops, of which wheat is the largest and most valuable. The prairies are often nicknamed "Canada's breadbasket" because almost all of Canada's grain crops are raised there. Millions of tons of wheat, oats, barley, soybeans, and sunflower seeds are grown in Manitoba, Saskatchewan, and Alberta each year.

Ontario and Québec, in the Central region, are the leaders in dairy farming. They also produce more poultry, sheep, hogs, fruits, vegetables, flowers, and tobacco than any other province. The Atlantic region, comprising New Brunswick and Prince Edward Island, is famous for its tasty potatoes.

Mineral Mining

Some of the world's richest mineral deposits are found in Canada. Mining is a huge industry: There are more than 300 mines across the country, with the highest concentration in Alberta, British Columbia, Québec,

Tourism

The majority of tourists who come to Canada are from the United States. They come to enjoy the country's vast open spaces and unspoiled beauty and take part in outdoor pursuits such as skiing, hiking, and kayaking. In recent years the Canadian Tourist Board has tried to attract more European tourists by emphasizing the country's diversity of cultures and the beauty of its older cities such as Montréal. The new Inuit territory of Nunavut hopes to develop the region's tourism to earn additional income.

MAIN TOURIST ARRIVALS

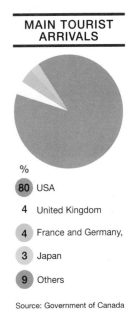

%
- **80** USA
- **4** United Kingdom
- **4** France and Germany,
- **3** Japan
- **9** Others

Source: Government of Canada

MAJOR INDUSTRIES

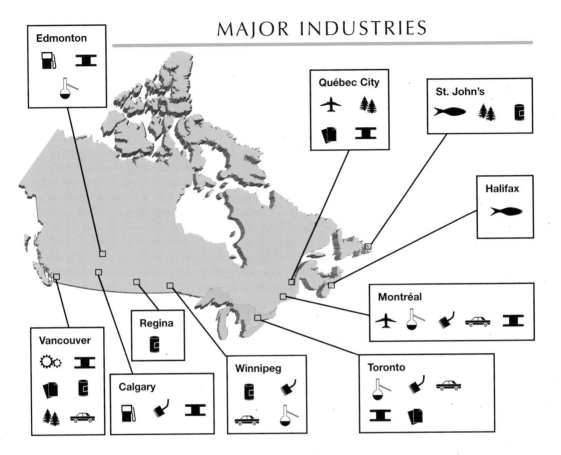

Edmonton

Québec City

St. John's

Halifax

Montréal

Vancouver

Regina

Calgary

Winnipeg

Toronto

Vehicle assembly

Electronics

Paper and pulp

Timber industries

Aerospace

Chemicals

Engineering

Metal working

Fisheries

Food processing

Oil and gas

The map above shows the most important industries found in Canada's major cities.

and Saskatchewan. Today the mining industry employs thousands of highly trained people in exploration, extraction, and refining.

Canada is the largest producer of zinc and asbestos and is second largest in the production of nickel, potash, sulfur, gypsum, uranium, and titanium. The country is ranked among the top five producers of gold, silver, platinum, molybdenum, cadmium, lead, and copper. Nearly 80 percent of Canada's minerals and mineral products are exported, mostly to the United States.

Although it is important to the economy, mining is also one of Canada's largest energy users and worst causes of pollution. Many Canadians blame mining for some of their country's environmental problems, including water and air pollution and the destruction of natural habitats and landscapes.

Manufacturing Industry

Canada is one of the top ten industrial countries in the world. About 60 percent of the country's manufacturing is located in the Great Lakes–St. Lawrence region of Ontario and Québec. This area has excellent water, rail, and road transportation (*see* pp. 90–92), plenty of energy and raw materials, and a huge section of the country's population, which provides a large workforce and local market to produce and buy the goods.

Fishing—An Industry in Decline?

With oceans on three sides and more fresh water than any other country in the world, Canadians once had one of the largest fishing industries. The recent depletion of fish populations, however, has led to an almost complete collapse of the industry. The Atlantic fishery (*see* p. 55), which includes the famous Grand Banks, was Canada's major fishing ground for centuries, until the major catch—cod—became so overfished that there were too few left to support the industry. In 1992 the Canadian government put a ban on cod fishing that has

In an attempt to stem the decline of the Pacific salmon stocks, the government has promoted the establishment of artificial spawning grounds such as this one, photographed from the air.

ENERGY SOURCES

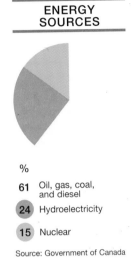

%	
61	Oil, gas, coal, and diesel
24	Hydroelectricity
15	Nuclear

Source: Government of Canada

Canada is one of the world's biggest producers and exporters of hydroelectricity. Much of the hydroelectricity produced in Québec supplies energy to the northeastern United States.

The first commercial oil well in North America was drilled in Enniskillen Township, near Sarnia, Ontario, in 1856.

continued to the present day. Since the Atlantic fishery collapsed, the government has endeavored to devise programs to help the 80,000 fish harvesters who have lost their jobs.

More than half the catch in the Pacific fishery is made up of Canadian Pacific salmon. This fish is a delicacy in many parts of the world, so it is very valuable. Fish harvesters and scientists are concerned, however, about shrinking salmon populations and fear that the Pacific fishery may collapse as the Atlantic one did.

A Wealth of Energy

The country has a wealth of energy sources, including oil, petroleum, natural gas, water for hydroelectricity, and uranium for nuclear power. Hydroelectricity is the cheapest type of energy, but oil and natural gas, used to heat buildings and run cars, trucks, and factories, play the largest role in meeting Canada's energy needs.

Canadians produce much more energy than they need, and extra energy and energy sources are sold to other countries. Alberta and Saskatchewan have been exporting oil for decades. Scientists believe there are still enormous amounts of oil yet to be tapped from the Earth deep beneath these provinces—more than in Saudi Arabia, Kuwait, and the United Arab Emirates combined. In 1997 production began at a new oil field, Hibernia, which is located off the coast of Newfoundland. Nunavut and the Northwest Territories also have largely untapped reserves of oil.

Electricity, coal, and uranium are also exported. The largest customer for Canadian energy is the United States, although Japan and other Pacific Rim countries also buy a great deal.

Although western Canada produces huge amounts of oil, Canada still imports crude oil from other countries because it is less expensive for Canadians in Atlantic Canada to import oil than to transport it thousands of miles from Western Canada.

Protecting the Environment

People around the world now recognize that industrial development has too often been bought at the cost of damaging the environment. The Earth Summits held in Rio de Janeiro, Brazil, in 1992, in Kyoto, Japan, in 1997, and in Buenos Aires, Argentina, in 1998, put forward a new approach to the environment in which economic growth and environmental concerns go hand in hand. This approach is called sustainable development.

Canada takes sustainable development very seriously and supports the directives of these three summits. There are moves to clean up the Great Lakes–St. Lawrence Seaway, which has become polluted by heavy industry. The government is also tackling the problem of acid rain—caused by emissions of carbon dioxide, sulfur dioxide, and nitrogen oxide from vehicles and industry.

In the early 1990s, Canada's rate of carbon-dioxide emissions were higher, at 4.5 short tons (4.1 t) per person per year, than those of France, Japan, and the former Soviet Union. Acid rain was degrading Canada's forests and rivers. In Nova Scotia fishing organizations put up signs like the one below warning people of the danger of acid rain and its toxic effect on rivers and salmon runs.

Canada is also trying to modify industrial and agricultural practices in the face of environmental concerns. Across the country, the government has established forest-management projects that stress the importance of planting as well as harvesting Canada's "green gold."

The government of Canada continues to set aside large areas of the country as protected space. Its network of national parks is one of the most impressive in the world (*see* p. 31) and is being expanded. The government has also taken action to protect one of the world's last untouched and most fragile environments—the Arctic north.

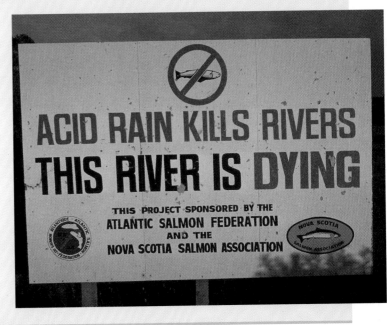

ACID RAIN KILLS RIVERS
THIS RIVER IS DYING

THIS PROJECT SPONSORED BY THE
ATLANTIC SALMON FEDERATION
AND THE
NOVA SCOTIA SALMON ASSOCIATION

TRANSPORTATION

Without a good transportation network, Canada could not have become a unified country. Until the mid-1800s, Canada was little more than a collection of isolated towns and villages. Getting from place to place was slow and difficult and often became impossible in winter. By the late 1800s, improved types of transportation were developed, and the problems of connecting the scattered settlements lessened. Today Canadians enjoy one of the best transportation systems in the world, made up of roads, highways, railroads, air routes, and waterways.

The Great Lakes–St. Lawrence Seaway was a great engineering feat. To overcome the 600-foot (183 m) drop between Lake Superior and the Atlantic Ocean, engineers devised a system of locks such as the one pictured below.

On the Water

After walking, traveling by water was the very earliest means of transportation in Canada. Native peoples used canoes to get around for centuries. When European explorers reached Canada in their ships, they used rivers to move inland. Water transportation played a vital part in the lives of early settlers. Boats carried their goods back to Europe and, more importantly, brought back necessary supplies. Until the mid-1800s, when roads and railroads were built across the country, waterways offered the fastest, easiest method of transportation.

The Great Lakes–St. Lawrence Seaway is made up of the five Great Lakes, the St. Lawrence River, and a series of locks and canals. It is the largest waterway in the world, stretching 2,342 miles (3,769 km) from the North American interior to the Atlantic Ocean. This vital transportation system is used to move materials to and from the industrial heartland of the United States and Canada.

TRANSPORTATION

Canada's road and rail networks are concentrated in the south, providing an east–west link between the country's major cities. The capitals of the territories—Whitehorse, Yellowknife, and Iqaluit—are isolated from the main communication network and are reached mostly by airplane.

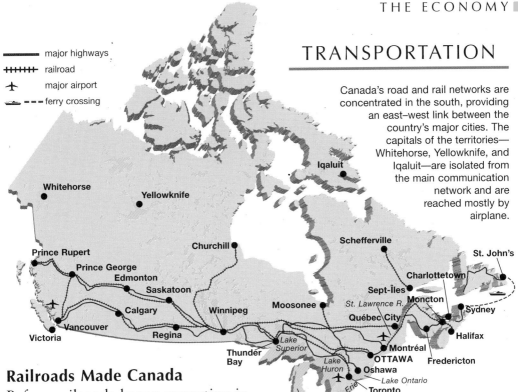

major highways
railroad
major airport
ferry crossing

Railroads Made Canada

Before railroads began operating in Canada, travel was slow, uncomfortable, and endured only when absolutely necessary. Roads were so rough that wagon wheels often broke, fell off, or stuck in the mud. Traveling by boat was more pleasant than by carriage, but waterways froze during the winter. Railroads were a faster, more comfortable, and convenient means of transportation. They became such an important link between Canadian communities that, by the early 20th century, Canada had more rail miles per capita than any other country in the world. Today the country has over 56,000 miles (90,000 km) of railroad tracks.

While water transportation helped start Canada's first industry—the fur trade—the railroad helped form the nation. It linked isolated settlements and allowed people, mail, crops, and other goods to be moved quickly and easily. The railroad

The Canadian Pacific Railway passes through some of the country's most breathtaking landscapes. Here a train passes through the dramatic Rockies.

The Snowmobile

In the 1950s the Canadian Joseph-Armand Bombardier developed the world's first snowmobile. The snowmobile is a lightweight motorized sled or toboggan that is used to get around in the snowy Canadian wilderness. The Inuit quickly adopted Bombardier's invention to do work that they had previously done with a dogsled. Mounties, too, use snowmobiles to police inaccessible areas of Canada's national parks, and they have proved indispensable for rescue work.

The Trans-Canada Highway is one of the longest paved roads in the world. It stretches almost 5,000 miles (8,050 km) from St. John's, Newfoundland, to Vancouver, British Columbia. This amazing feat of engineering was started in 1950 and took 20 years to build.

was such an important link that the province of British Columbia would not agree to join the confederation (*see* pp. 65–67) until the other provinces guaranteed that a railroad would be built connecting British Columbia to the other provinces. When this cross-country railroad, called the Canadian Pacific Railway, was finally completed in 1885, it was the longest in the world.

Because increasing numbers of people are using automobiles or airplanes to travel in Canada, the country's railroads are now in something of a decline. In 1990 the government cut back passenger services on the railroads by more than half. Today the legendary "Canadian" train that once went daily from Montréal to Vancouver departs only three times a week and then only from Toronto.

"Have car, will travel"

Canadians love to drive. They operate more than 13 million cars and over three million trucks and buses. More than 80 percent of all travel in Canada is on roads and highways. Most of these are located in the southern part of the nation—more than 559,000 miles (900,000 km). Canada's sparsely populated north has very few roads compared to the south.

Air Travel

In 1937 Canada's first passenger airline began offering flights between Montréal, Ottawa, Toronto, and Vancouver. Today every major city has an international airport. Many smaller cities have airports offering flights to the United States. Canada's busiest airport is Pearson International Airport in Toronto.

Since Canada is such an enormous country, airplanes are often the most efficient means of traveling around it. Hundreds of flights leave airports across Canada every hour. Jets can move passengers from Vancouver to Halifax in just seven hours—a trip that would take several days on the ground. Small planes and helicopters are a necessary part of life in the remote north where there are no roads.

COMMUNICATION SYSTEMS

As a huge, industrialized nation, Canada needs a widespread, quick system of transferring information. Canadians have one of the largest and most sophisticated communications systems in the world. Besides their postal service, they use satellites, telephones, computers, and radios to send messages. This system helps Canadian businesses and industries run efficiently, allows family and friends to stay in touch, and enables rescue workers to respond quickly to emergencies. Inuit communities rely on the Internet to communicate with other remote settlements.

Long-distance

Scottish-born Alexander Graham Bell (1847–1922) conceived the idea for the telephone in 1874 while living in Brantford, Ontario. Although Bell actually built the first telephone in Boston in 1875, he made the first building-to-building call in Mt. Pleasant, Ontario, in 1876. One week later he placed the first long-distance call from Brantford to Paris, Ontario.

The first long-distance radio message was received in St. John's, Newfoundland, in 1901. The Italian inventor Guglielmo Marconi (1874–1937) sent the signal across the Atlantic Ocean from Britain, using a transmitter he had built.

Arts and Living

"What must astonish most is to see paintings everywhere, everywhere sculpture, among a nation of hunters."

French captain Marchand, in 1801, describing the art of the Northwest Coast

At first glance the lifestyles of Canadians can seem very similar to those of their neighbors in the United States. On both sides of the border, people work, eat, and spend their leisure time in much the same way. They watch a lot of the same TV programs and like the same sports, including baseball, soccer, and hockey.

However, Canada's vast area means that there are strong regional identities. A journey from Canada's east coast to its west coast would reveal an enormous diversity of lifestyles. The often rugged life of Newfoundlanders has little in common with that of the easygoing Vancouverites, while the lifestyle of Québec City, with its emphasis on good food and good living, can even seem to belong to a different continent altogether.

Moreover, Canada has an incredible wealth of cultural traditions—as even a brief walk around Toronto's multiethnic downtown reveals. Canadians are proud of the way in which both immigrant and Native peoples have successfully maintained traditional ways of living within the larger context of Canada.

Nevertheless, many Canadians worry about the overwhelming influence of U.S. culture on their country. They point to the large numbers of Canadian artists and musicians who leave to work in the United States. Their concern is part of a broader question about what it means to be Canadian and how this differs from being American.

In winter Ottawa's Rideau Canal freezes over, and the city's inhabitants take to the ice. Above the canal are the Canadian parliament buildings.

Animal transformation masks like this one were used during the potlatch ceremony. Dancers acted out stories about the courage of a family ancestor who was able to enter the animal domain and bring back wealth for his family. A system of levers and pulleys allowed the dancer to reveal a new mask and "change shape" from animal to human and back again.

ARTS, LITERATURE, AND MUSIC

The arts have thrived in Canada for centuries, but it is only within the past few decades that Canadians have begun to make a cultural impact not just in Canada but throughout the world. Today the government actively encourages the growth of the arts, and Canadians enjoy a mixture of home-grown and international film, television, music, and other creative arts.

Sculpture and Painting

People in Canada have been skillfully creating crafts and works of art for centuries. Such works were not only art in the modern sense—that is, objects to be admired for their beauty or skill—but usually had a ritual or religious significance, too. The Native peoples of the Northwest Coast, where there was a good supply of cedar and spruce, created some of the finest wooden sculptures of

Native North America. The most spectacular were the crest, or "totem," poles that were carved from cedar trunks as high as 60 feet (18 m). The poles were often placed outside family houses and displayed ancestral crests—depictions of animals such as the beaver, bear, salmon, whale, or raven that showed the family's origins.

The Inuit created fine carvings of seals, bears, fish, and people. The carvings were usually made out of bone, tooth, or tusk and often reflected a unique sense of humor as well as a high degree of skill.

Today First Nations communities and the Inuit continue to practice traditional crafts such as carving, print-making, and weaving. Although much is now produced for the tourist market, works of great power continue to be created, sometimes fusing Native and European elements. Important Native artists include the Haida sculptor Bill Reid (1920–1998) and the Inuit print-maker Jessie Oonark (born 1906).

European immigrant artists usually worked in the traditions of their home countries. By the late 19th century, however, a distinctive Canadian art developed that was in large part a response to the beauty of the Canadian landscape. In the 1920s the Group of Seven set out to produce brilliantly colored paintings that reflected Canadian themes and concerns. Closely associated with the Group of Seven was Emily Carr, who worked on Canada's west coast (*see* p. 98).

From the 1930s many artists experimented with international movements such as abstraction, in which painting concerns itself with color and form but does not attempt to show objects as they are. Even today, however, realistic subjects remain popular, as in the work of wildlife painter Robert Bateman.

Telling Stories

The Native North Americans had no written alphabet. Folk stories were passed orally—by word of mouth—down through the generations. Storytellers were often

Scholars often compare Native crests to the "coats of arms" used by the European nobility. Both the crests and coats of arms could only be used by their rightful owners—powerful families who controlled land and resources.

Emily Carr

Emily Carr (1871–1945) is one of Canada's best-loved painters. She grew up in British Columbia, but at the beginning of the 20th century, she went to Paris, France. There she fell under the spell of the vibrant colors and emotional intensity of French artists such as André Derain and Henri Matisse.

After returning to Vancouver, Carr made frequent trips to sketch the Native villages and wild landscapes of British Columbia. Her work showed big, bold landscapes and sympathetic depictions of Native life but was largely ignored by both critics and the public.

In 1927 Carr found fresh inspiration after seeing the work of the Group of Seven in an exhibition in Toronto. Her own work, such as the painting above of a totem pole on Graham Island in British Columbia, became popular and began to fetch high prices.

Toward the end of her life, poor health put an end to her sketching tours. Instead she turned her hand to writing a series of funny, moving autobiographies.

important and respected members of society. They told their stories at night around the campfire and changed the stories to suit their taste and humor.

As in the fine arts, it was a long time before the English- and French-speaking Canadians developed a modern literature that was distinctively Canadian. In the 1940s a new generation of novelists emerged.

Robertson Davies (1913–1995) was an actor and playwright who also wrote long, complex novels that often include beautiful descriptions evoking life in Canada at the beginning of the 20th century. The Montréal-based Mordecai Richler (born 1931) writes stories that are rooted in his childhood in the Jewish, working-class district of Montréal.

Many of the best-known Canadian writers working today are women. In her moving short stories, Alice Munro (born 1931) often depicts small-town communities in her native Ontario, while the novels of Margaret Atwood (born 1939) explore feminist and environmental concerns. In her book *Surfacing* the heroine goes in search of her lost father in the Canadian wilderness and gains strength from her renewed contact with nature. In such novels as *Happenstance*, *The Stone Diaries*, and *Larry's Party*, Carol Shields (born 1935) celebrates and makes extraordinary the lives of ordinary Canadian men and women.

"In Flanders Fields"

John McCrae (1872–1918) was a Canadian doctor who began writing poetry while studying at McGill University in Montréal. In 1914 he volunteered to fight in World War I as a gunner but later worked as a doctor. He wrote his best-known poem, "In Flanders Fields," in 1915, when people were still enthusiastic about the war. Flanders is a region of France and Belgium where many of the war's battles were fought. McCrae died of pneumonia in 1918. His poem became one of the most famous poems of the war.

In Flanders fields the poppies blow
Between the crosses, row on row
That mark our place; and in the sky
The larks, still bravely singing, fly
Scarce heard amid the guns below.

We are the Dead. Short days ago
We lived, felt dawn, saw sunset glow,
Loved and were loved, and now
    we lie
In Flanders fields.

Take up our quarrel with the foe:
To you from failing hands we throw
The torch; be yours to hold it high.
If ye break faith with us who die
We shall not sleep, though
    poppies grow
In Flanders fields.

One of Canada's most famous literary characters was created by author Lucy Maud Montgomery (1874–1942). Her creation, Anne Shirley, appears in *Anne of Green Gables* (written in 1908) and other novels set in Prince Edward Island (*see* pp. 21–22), which have entertained readers worldwide since the early 1900s.

Canada's Folklore

Canadians share a wealth of folklore with origins from around the world. Of the folklore that originated in Canada, some of the best-known is that of the First Nations, Inuit, and French Canadians. Native peoples, for example, tell many stories about a mischievous hero called Raven. He was born at the edge of the world "in the north beyond the north" and could take the form of a bird or a human.

Raven stole the sun, moon, and stars for the people, who were cold and living in darkness. He tricked Snowy Owl into giving him fire and brought it back to the people. One day he vanished back into the north. An Inuit sculptor carved this raven mask for ceremonial use as a way of honoring their helpful hero.

One of the most popular French-Canadian stories, "Chasse-galerie," is portrayed in artwork and song. It had a different ending each time it was told. In this story the devil comes to a band of homesick *voyageurs* (*see* p. 60) in the wilderness, offering to fly them all the way home to Montréal overnight. He warns them that if they speak a single word during the flight, he will claim their souls forever.

The *voyageurs* accept the offer and hop in their canoe, which soars high into the sky. The *voyageurs* want to exclaim at the wondrous ride and the sight of the Earth far below, but remember their bargain and hold their tongues. When they finally see their homes ahead, the *voyageurs* desperately try to contain their excitement, as the devil waits for them to cry out in joy…

How do you think the story ends?

Televison, Radio, and Film

The Canadian Broadcasting Corporation (CBC) is Canada's government-funded radio and television network, which broadcasts both in English and French. It was formed in 1936 to broadcast news to people across the country and promote a sense of national unity. Since its creation the CBC has entertained Canadians with music, comedy, drama, and its most popular show, *Hockey Night in Canada*. Countless technicians and artists, many of whom have moved on to work in the United States, started out producing work for the CBC.

For about a century, Canadians have been making films both in Canada and abroad, although Canadian filmmakers have always been overshadowed by America's huge Hollywood film industry. In 1939 the Canadian government established the National Film Board (NFB) to "promote the production and distribution of films in the nation and…to interpret Canada to Canadians and to other countries."

Over the past 60 years, the NFB has assisted with funding and helped filmmakers produce their projects and develop their talents. As a result Canada today has a worldwide reputation for high-quality movies, documentaries, and animation shorts.

Important Canadian filmmakers working today include Denys Arcand (born 1941), who makes films about contemporary life in Montréal, and Atom Egoyan (born 1960), who makes highly controversial movies, such as *The Sweet Here-after*, about the dehumanizing effects of society and media such as video, television, and film itself.

It may come as a surprise to know that Hollywood star Jim Carrey is Canadian-born. Often a famous Canadian's nationality is not known to his or her American fans.

Superman, a world-renowned symbol of American justice and heroism, was co-created by a Canadian, Joe Schuster. Schuster based the city of Metropolis on Toronto, his hometown, and the *Daily Planet*, on a Toronto newspaper.

Keeping Canadian Culture Canadian

The issue of "Americanization" is especially of concern to people in Canada's music, film, television, and publishing industries. Given the huge size and wealth of these industries in the United States, many Canadians feel that their industries cannot compete. One has only to look at how many Canadian performers have moved to the United States to further their careers to realize that some fear for Canadian culture may be justified. For example, present-day actors Mike Myers, Jim Carrey, Keanu Reeves, Dan Aykroyd, and Pamela Anderson are all Canadian-born.

The Canadian government established the Canadian Radio and Television Commission (CRTC) to help Canadian music and television programming compete with that of the United States. Under CRTC standards, radio and television stations broadcasting out of Canada must include at least 30 percent Canadian content in their programming.

A World-class Theater

After London and New York, Toronto enjoys the reputation of being the world's third-largest center for English-language theater productions and has hosted hit musicals such as *The Phantom of the Opera*, *Les Misèrables*, *Joseph and the Amazing Technicolor Dreamcoat*, and *Rent*.

Montréal is a world leader in French theater and boasts renowned experimental artists such as writer-director and filmmaker Robert Lepage (born 1957) and Michel Tremblay (born 1955), who writes plays in the local French Canadian dialect known as *joual*. Playwrights Judith Thompson (born 1954) and Tomson Highway have won critical acclaim for their powerful and amusing dramas about life in Canada.

One of Canada's most famous theater companies is Cirque de Soleil ("Circus of the Sun"). Since 1984 it has delighted audiences across the world with its lively

Montréal is famous for its exciting and innovative dance companies, such as Les Ballets Jazz de Montréal and Les Grands Ballets Canadiens. Every other year the city holds an international festival of new dance.

blend of circus, music, and drama. The famous Stratford Festival, in Ontario, holds the biggest festival of William Shakespeare's plays in the world outside England, while children's theater is the specialty of many companies including Green Thumb, Les Deux Mondes ("The Two Worlds"), and Theatre Beyond Words.

The Stratford Festival—held from May to late October—attracts some 500,000 people every year.

Native Music

Canada has a great variety of folk musical traditions, both Native American and European. The Inuit people, for example, have a rich tradition of vocal music that accompanies ceremonies such as the launching of a new boat. Singers make an astonishing range of noises, including shouts, animal-like cries, and tongue-clicking. Inuit singers are often accompanied by drums, rattles,

The Wayward Genius of Glen Gould

Glen Gould (1932–1982) was one of Canada's most famous and most eccentric musicians (*right*). This brilliant piano player hated Mozart, stayed awake all night and slept all day, and never shook hands because he was afraid his fingers would be damaged. One conductor famously said of him: "The nut's a genius!" while a critic described him as "a young man in a kind of trance."

At the age of 32, Gould gave up concert performances altogether and made recordings only, which he did in a studio specially built for him in Eaton's department store in Toronto. His most famous recording was his first, Bach's *Goldberg Variations*, which continues to be a best-seller.

and bullroarers. A bullroarer is a flat piece of wood or bone with a jagged edge that is attached to a piece of string. The player whirls the instrument around his or her head to make a hypnotic rhythm. As the Inuit came into contact with the European settlers, they made new instruments, including simple stringed ones such as the so-called Eskimo (Inuit) violin.

Music of the Immigrants

The first French and British settlers brought with them the songs, rhythms, and instruments of their homelands. In the 18th and 19th centuries, the boatmen-traders, called *voyageurs,* made their long, hard journeys more lively by singing. Their songs—called *chansons d'aviron* (rowing songs)—were often very long, sometimes with as many as 50 or 60 verses. They told stories about love or the sadness of leaving France. The songs' rhythms matched the *voyageurs'* paddle strokes.

To make this drum, an Inuit craftsman stretched a seal's bladder over a sprucewood frame.

Settlers from England, Scotland, and Ireland on the remote islands of Newfoundland, Nova Scotia, and Cape Breton Island adapted their native traditions to their new environment. Living in isolated villages, they had to entertain themselves. An evening dance was often accompanied by a fiddler and button accordionist or by "chin music"—a singer, with his hand resting on his chin and cheek, repeating sounds in a rhythmic way.

Newfoundland's singers, though, often performed alone, without accompaniment. Their moving, simple ballads were about lost love or the hardships of the seafaring life. Because the songs and melodies were not written down but passed on from generation to generation, the singers and instrumentalists often improvised, and over the years each village and region developed its own particular style of playing and singing.

In the 20th century, some of these musical traditions began to be lost with the introduction of musical styles from the United States, such as country and western or the blues. Scholars have worked hard to preserve traditional Canadian songs, and many younger musicians, such as fiddler Ashley MacIsaac, are today reviving the old styles or looking to the past for inspiration in writing new music.

The fiddler Ashley MacIsaac reinterprets traditional Canadian music for new, young audiences.

Today virtually every style of music is played. Rock, country, folk, and jazz are the most popular genres, and such Canadian singers as Joni Mitchell, Jane Siberry, k.d. lang, Alanis Morissette, Céline Dion, Neil Young, Bryan Adams, and jazz pianist Oscar Peterson are known worldwide for their talents.

DAILY LIFE

Like almost everyone else in the world, Canadians center their lives around family, friends, and work. Most Canadian families are made up of parents and their children, but a growing number are headed by a single parent. In many ways daily life in Canada is much like that in the United States or Europe. After spending the day at school or work, most people return home to share dinner with their family.

Although some Canadians earn extra money by working in the evening or on weekends, others spend their free time enjoying the outdoors, playing sports, pursuing hobbies, attending cultural events, watching television or movies, or exploring the Internet.

"You have to know a man awfully well in Canada to know his surname." Governor-General John Buchan

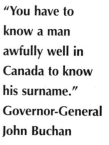

Education

Education is an important part of life in Canada. The emphasis placed on education is reflected in the fact that the Canadian provincial governments collectively spend 7.6 percent of gross national product (GNP) on funding schools and universities. The United States spends less on education, some 5.3 percent of GNP.

One thing almost all Canadian children have in common is that, Monday to Friday, from September to June, they are busy in school. Most students spend six or seven years in an elementary school, before completing three to five years of secondary education in a high school.

Each province has its own system of public elementary and high schools, which are coeducational. Ontario, Alberta, and Québec also offer "separate" schools, which, unlike public schools, include religion as part of the education. Most separate schools are Roman Catholic.

Students at elementary school learn language, math, science, social studies, arts, and physical education. High schools offer the same subjects, as well as many extracurricular activities and events such as theater, music programs, clubs, and sports. In order to help promote bilingualism, English-speaking students must take French classes, and French speakers must take lessons in English. Some schools are fully bilingual.

After completing high school at the age of 17 or 18, students often continue their education at a university or college, where they specialize in fields such as the arts, business, or science. Unlike elementary and secondary education, university learning is not free, but many students

ATTENDANCE AT SCHOOL

Level	Percentage
College and university	70%
High school	93%
Elementary	100%

This chart shows the percentage of Canadians who attend each level of education.

The ivy-clad Hart House, part of the University of Toronto, Ontario, evokes the renowned English universities of Oxford and Cambridge. The tower commemorates Canadian soldiers who died in World War I and is inscribed with John McCrae's poem "In Flanders Fields."

receive government assistance to help pay for their tuition. Some 70 percent of high-school students go on to study at a university or college—the highest proportion in the world.

Health and Medicine

Canada is ranked among the countries with the highest standards of living, so it is not surprising that Canada boasts one of the best medical and health systems in the world. The government spends almost 10 percent of GNP on health services, such as hospitals and family doctors.

All Canadians have free access to health care, which means visits to a doctor or hospital are free of charge. The only health service not paid for, at least in part, by the government is a visit to the dentist. Most senior citizens and people receiving social assistance also have most of their prescription drugs paid for by the government. As a result the Canadian people enjoy longer life expectancies than almost any other people in the world.

Food from All Over the World

When it comes to mealtime, Canadians have a wide variety of choices, from lobster, fish, and shrimp to grains and cereals, fruits and vegetables, chicken, beef, and pork, and more unusual meats such as bear, moose, and caribou. Markets, grocery stores, and restaurants reflect the cultural mosaic of Canadian society, offering dishes and ingredients typical of European, Asian, Jewish, African, Caribbean, and Middle Eastern cooking.

HOW CANADIANS SPEND THEIR MONEY

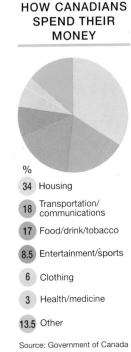

%	
34	Housing
18	Transportation/communications
17	Food/drink/tobacco
8.5	Entertainment/sports
6	Clothing
3	Health/medicine
13.5	Other

Source: Government of Canada

The chart above shows how the average Canadian household divides up its expenditures. Canadian families spend a great deal of their income on their homes and on keeping them well decorated and warm.

WHAT DO CANADIANS OWN?

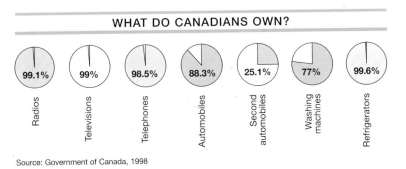

Radios	Televisions	Telephones	Automobiles	Second automobiles	Washing machines	Refrigerators
99.1%	99%	98.5%	88.3%	25.1%	77%	99.6%

Source: Government of Canada, 1998

These charts shows the percentage of Canadian households that own major consumer products.

A man in a horse-drawn sleigh collects maple sap. The trees are tapped and the sap collected in early spring when snow is often still on the ground.

There are strong regional variations in diet as well. New Brunswick, for example, is famous for its fiddleheads (fern shoots) and seaweed dishes. Newfoundland is famous for its fresh local fish; Nova Scotia for its scallops, blueberries, and apple dumplings. Saskatchewan and Manitoba are known for their freshwater fish, such as goldeye. In Québec there are pork dishes, such as *creton* (spicy pork pâté) and *tourtière* (minced-pork pie).

Maple Syrup

The most famous Canadian flavoring is maple syrup. Native peoples first showed French settlers how to tap maple trees (*see* p. 6) for their sap, which flows in the early spring. After hours of boiling, or "sugaring off," the sap becomes sweet maple sugar and syrup, which then can be used to flavor a variety of foods, from meats and beans to desserts.

Deep in the Québec countryside, there are places called *cabânes à sucre*— sugar shacks—that serve up maple syrup in all kinds of ways.

One of the most popular dishes using maple syrup is *trempette*, which is easy to make at home. This simple dish is made by soaking bread in maple syrup and serving it with lots of fresh cream.

A Diversity of Beliefs

Canada is home to a multitude of religions and beliefs. Christians, Jews, Muslims, Sikhs, Buddhists, Hindus, and atheists live alongside each another with remarkable tolerance. The majority of Canadians, however, are Christian. Almost half of the population is Roman Catholic, and about one-quarter is Protestant.

Many of these people, however, do not practice their religion on a daily basis. In fact, regular attendance at a place of worship is declining for all religions in Canada. The number of Canadians who claim to have no religious belief is increasing.

With so many religions present in Canada, and with Canadians practicing their chosen religion to different degrees, there is no one typical daily religious ritual. Some Canadians may incorporate aspects of their faith into their activities every day, while others attend their place of worship once or twice a month or only once a year.

Festivals and Celebrations

Canadians love to have a good time, as their many festivals, celebrations, and holidays illustrate. The national holiday, Canada Day, is observed on July 1. It celebrates the day in 1867 when the first provinces formed the confederation (*see* pp. 65–67). Most Canadians have a vacation from work, and holiday festivities typically include picnics, barbecues, and fireworks. Labor Day, celebrated the first Monday in September, is a day that honors the labor force. November 11 marks Remembrance Day, a somber holiday on which Canadians honor soldiers who fought and died for Canada in World War I (*see* p. 69) and later conflicts.

Bonhomme Carnival

Québec City, nicknamed the "Snow Capital of the World," has hosted a winter carnival every year since 1955. The festival celebrates the wonders of winter and includes exhibits of ice sculptures, a canoe race across the St. Lawrence River, dogsled races, night parades, and many other activities involving fun with ice or snow. One of the best-known features is the carnival's mascot, a huge snowman named Bonhomme ("good guy"), whose home is a palace made of ice. More than 60,000 people come into Québec City from elsewhere, and hundreds of thousands take part in the carnival.

In Québec there is a holiday for St. Jean-Baptiste (St. John the Baptist), the patron saint of Québec and Canada. He became the patron saint because John Cabot (*see* p. 54) landed on the coast of eastern Canada on June 24—the feast of St. John the Baptist—in 1497.

In small towns and big cities alike, hundreds of festivals are held throughout the year to celebrate everything

The Calgary Stampede

For ten days every July, Calgarians welcome hundreds of thousands of tourists as they stage the world's largest outdoor rodeo—the Calgary Stampede. The event takes place in Stampede Park on the southeastern edge of downtown Calgary. During the stampede the cowpoke lifestyle rules, as people dress in typical Western gear to enjoy barbecues, chuckwagon races, and the dozens of team and individual rodeo competitions. Calgary's Half Million Dollar Rodeo is the largest purse offered in the sport.

from the season to the performing arts. Festivals held in towns and small cities often celebrate local industry, such as a certain agricultural product or arts and crafts. Some of Canada's larger festivals are known throughout the world and attract visitors and artists from many other countries. These international celebrations include the annual Montréal Jazz Festival, International Fireworks Competition, and the Toronto Film Festival, which is the third-largest movie festival in the world.

Canadians take pride in their cultural and ethnic diversity, and most cities, large or small, hold festivals to celebrate multiculturalism. These festivals offer people the chance to learn more about other cultures, as they sample the food, watch the dancing, and listen to the music of different ethnic groups.

National Holidays and Festivals	
January 1	New Year's Day
March/April	Good Friday
March/April	Easter Monday
Third Monday in May	Victoria Day
July 1	Canada Day
First Monday in September	Labor Day
Second Monday in October	Thanksgiving
December 25	Christmas Day
December 26	Boxing Day

Wild About Shopping

Canadians have a wide variety of stores at which to indulge their love of shopping. Many prefer to visit their local mall or department store, where they find convenient parking and a large selection of goods under one roof. Downtown streets are also lined with busy strip malls and small, family-owned stores. A few Canadians satisfy their urge to shop by watching shopping channels and ordering goods by phone or via the Internet.

The huge West Edmonton Mall is the world's largest. It sprawls over the equivalent of 115 football fields or 48 city blocks. It has some 800 shops, 110 restaurants, 19 movie theaters, and 11 department stores. There is even a water park, where there are rides in submarines. The mall employs 15,000 people and attracts 55,000 customers a day.

How to Say...

Canadians speak many different languages. Among Native languages, that of the Inuit, Inuktitut, is the most widely spoken, and in multiethnic cities such as Toronto, it is possible to hear languages from all over the globe. Most natives and immigrants, however, speak one of Canada's two official languages—French and English.

Canadian French, or Québécois, differs from European French somewhat as American English differs from British English. Québécois tends to be less formal than French, and quite a few words are different. Most of all, though, it is the pronunciation of Québécois that sets the language apart from European French. For example, the French phrase for "not at all," *pas de tout,* pronounced *pa[r]-de[r]-too* in France, is pronounced *pan toot* in Québec. However, Canada's French-speakers are glad when an American tries to speak French at all—no matter what kind!

Below are a few French phrases, together with a pronunciation guide that follows the language as it is spoken in France. Many sounds are pronounced nasally (in the nose)—this is indicated in the pronunciation guide by a square bracket ([ ]). The French also roll their r's slightly. *Bonne chance*—good luck!

Please   *S'il vous plaît* (seel-voo-play)

Thank you   *Merci* (ma[re]-see)

Yes   *Oui* (wee)   No   *Non* (no[n])

Hello   *Bonjour* (boh[n]-zhur)

Goodbye   *Au revoir* (oh-rev-ooar)

How are you?   *Ça va?* (sa va)

Sorry   *Pardon* (par-doh[n])

Do you speak English?   *Vous parlez l'anglais?* (voo-par-lay lo[n]-glay)?

I don't understand   *Je ne comprends pas* (zhe[r]-ne-kom-pro[n]-pa)

What is your name?   *Comment vous-appelez-vous* (kom-o[n]-vooz-ap-play-voo)

My name is...   *Je m'appelle...* (zhe[r] ma-pel...)

Numbers/Les *nombres*:

One   *un/une* (uh[n]/oon)

Two   *deux* (de[r])

Three   *trois* (twah)

Four   *quatre* (kat-[re])

Five   *cinq* (sank)

Six   *six* (sees)

Seven   *sept* (set)

Eight   *huit* (wee[t])

Nine   *neuf* (nehf)

Ten   *dix* (dees)

Days of the week/*Les jours de la semaine*:

Monday   *lundi* (lun-dee)

Tuesday   *mardi* (mar-dee)

Wednesday   *mercredi* (merk-r[ay]-dee)

Thursday   *jeudi* (zhe[r]-dee)

Friday   *vendredi* (ve[n]-d[re]-dee)

Saturday   *samedi* (sam-[eh]-dee)

Sunday   *dimanche* (dee-m[on]sh)

Urban and Rural Contrasts

There are many differences between lifestyles in Canada's urban and rural areas. The majority of Canadians live in towns and cities that are close to a range of stores, services, and leisure facilities. In the largest cities, there are diverse cultural programs and events. Many people live in high-rises and other apartments or attached houses, where living space can be small and neighbors seemingly countless. In general, life is fast-paced. Despite extensive public transit systems, streets are very busy with traffic, especially during the peak hours when people are traveling to and from work.

Canadians in rural areas, by contrast, enjoy a much quieter lifestyle. They are often employed in agriculture or another industry, such as mining, and have a close relationship with their few neighbors. Buildings are much farther apart, roads are far from crowded, and the pace of life is much slower. Despite many of these differences, however, rural Canadians often have daily routines and standards of living similar to city dwellers, and they are able to experience a wide variety of cultural events through television, radio, and other media.

Recreation and Sports

There are almost countless choices when it comes to spending leisure time. Besides shopping and watching television, Canadians often get together with friends and family to share conversation, food, and games. Movies are particularly popular, seen both in theaters and at home on the VCR.

Sports play a major part in daily life. Spectators can watch sports on television or at one of the country's countless arenas, fields, and gymnasiums. During the winter, hockey is Canada's roughest, fastest, and most popular sport. Almost half a million children and teens play hockey in organized leagues, and many more play on backyard rinks. The game is so popular that children play it even during the summer, when there is, of course,

Canadian James Naismith invented basketball while teaching a gym class in Springfield, Massachusetts, in 1891. He invented the game because his students needed an indoor game to play between the football and baseball seasons.

no ice. This game of "street hockey" is played using a ball instead of a puck, and players wear shoes or roller blades instead of skates.

Other popular winter sports include ice-skating, snowboarding, downhill and cross-country skiing, and curling, which is something like bowling on ice. The players slide a large stone that is fitted with a handle along the ice, trying to reach the center of the "house," which is a series of circles marked on the ice.

The National Sport: Lacrosse

Most people are surprised to learn that lacrosse—not hockey—is Canada's national sport. The Iroquois peoples of what is now Ontario and upper New York State were the first to play the game. They called it *baggataway*. It could be extremely rough and was almost like a war. Sometimes as many as a thousand players took part on each side. The goals were set three miles (5 km) apart, and games could last up to three days. Players used long-handled sticks with a triangular net pocket at the end to catch and throw the ball. When the French settlers first saw the game, the sticks reminded them of a bishop's crosier—*la crosse* in French—which gave the sport its modern name.

In the 19th century, French settlers adopted the game, initially playing against native teams. George Beers of Montréal was the first to lay down the rules of modern lacrosse. He limited teams to 12 members, replaced the native leather ball with a rubber one, and redesigned the crosse so that players could catch and throw the ball more easily.

Hockey's Greats

Perhaps the greatest Canadian hockey player of all time is Wayne Gretzky (born 1961; *right*) from Ontario. He has played for professional teams in Edmonton, Los Angeles, St. Louis, and New York and holds almost every record in the National Hockey League. His abilities to handle the puck and to shoot and pass with surefire accuracy have made him a legend. He retired from sport in 1999, having scored 894 goals and made 1,963 assists.

Before Wayne Gretzky, other famous Canadian hockey players included Bobby Orr, Jean Beliveau, and Gordon ("Gordie") Howe. Jean Beliveau (born 1932) was nicknamed "Le Gros Bill" ("Big Bill") and scored more than 500 goals. Gordie Howe (born 1928) spent 25 seasons in the National Hockey League.

Canada's abundant rivers, lakes, and beaches provide ideal locations for many summertime sports, such as swimming, fishing, and boating. Field sports such as baseball and football are extremely popular, as are track and field, bicycling, and soccer.

Two baseball teams, the Blue Jays and Montréal Expos, are included in the American major league baseball conferences. In 1993 and 1994, the Blue Jays became national heroes when they won the World Series twice in a row.

The Future

"Native people will have much to contribute over the next century. It's our turn."

George Erasmus, leader of the Assembly of First Nations, in 1986

Overall the outlook for Canadians in the 21st century is very bright. Their country has the stability, infrastructure, resources, and skilled citizens to maintain a good quality of life and remain an important influence in both world politics and the international economy. Canada's future, however, will not be without serious social, economic, and political challenges. Canadians must overcome the regional differences that threaten their country's unity and work together to face the challenges and opportunities offered in the new millennium.

CANADA'S STRENGTHS
The strengths that made Canada a world leader in the 20th century will continue to keep it at the center of world trade, politics, and culture well into the 21st century. Internationally Canada's respected voice will continue to play a leading role in advising world organizations such as NATO and the UN and in spearheading humanitarian efforts such as the International Treaty on Land Mines.

One of Canada's greatest sources of wealth has been its natural resources. Minerals and energy sources are still abundant, and government and industry must continue to investigate ways to develop them responsibly.

As manufacturing industries continue to move to other countries to cut costs, Canada's economy is becoming increasingly service-oriented and concentrated in

The traditional meets the modern—this Inuit man, who wears his people's traditional clothing of seal furs, uses a laptop to help run his business.

FACT FILE
- Canada prides itself on being a "community of communities," but there are doubts that its government will continue to be able to hold such a huge and disparate nation together.

- Canada must address tensions in its relationship with the United States. For example, there has been no agreement on restricting pollution from U.S. factories, responsible for much of the acid rain affecting Canada's forests.

- Canadians, who are used to high standards of welfare and free health care, look likely to suffer government spending cuts.

Canadian troops play an important role in United Nations (UN) peacekeeping missions throughout the world. These soldiers were among Canadian troops deployed in Bosnia, formerly part of Yugoslavia.

profitable high-tech industries. To do these jobs, Canada needs to continue to produce a well-trained workforce.

CANADA'S WEAKNESSES

As with its strengths, Canada has weaknesses that will follow it from the 20th century into the 21st. The mistrust and infighting between Canada's different regions, which has been a part of Canadian politics since before confederation, may overshadow other pressing issues such as child poverty and the environment.

The constant disagreement between federal and provincial levels of government regarding the funding of key programs such as health care and education must be resolved or these programs will continue to suffer cutbacks. Canadians worry that, while their politicians bicker, citizens will suffer the effects of a disintegrating welfare system. Canadians value highly their universal health-care system because it ensures that everyone, no matter how rich or poor, receives the same level of medical care.

Canadians are also worried that their government's poor management of natural resources, notably shown in the collapse of the Atlantic fisheries, may lead to further problems. Of particular concern are: the Pacific coast salmon fisheries, where there has been a decrease in salmon stocks; the delicate tundra ecosystems in the far north, where oil companies have proposed building drilling rigs; and the freshwater resources of the Great Lakes, which are being polluted by cities and industry.

THREATS TO CANADA

Perhaps the most serious threats to Canada's future come from within. The continuing popularity of separatism in Québec threatens to throw the country into political crisis. Many Canadians fear that the rest of Canada would not be able to survive without Québec as a part of the confederation.

Some Canadians are concerned, too, that while progress has been made in recent years, the government will continue to neglect the well-being of Native American groups. They also fear that some of the most contested land claims may lead to armed confrontations such as the one that occurred on Oka, Québec, in 1990.

There are only a few external threats to Canada. Because the Canadian economy relies heavily on exports, how well it performs is linked directly to the performance of its main markets, such as the United States and Japan, where it sells many of its products. Troubles in the economies of these countries can cause a loss of jobs and other problems in Canada. In addition, as the threat of rapid climate change looms in the wake of atmospheric pollution, some Canadians also worry that they may lose their productive farmland and forests.

NEW OPPORTUNITIES

The new century presents many opportunities for Canada to settle long-standing national problems and continue to set trends and distinguish itself internationally in the fields of peacekeeping, social programs, cultural tolerance, and environmental protection.

Despite past failures, most Canadians are optimists with the will to change and renew their country and to make Québécois, Native Americans, and other groups more content. Canada will also have the chance to improve and rebuild its social welfare to make sure all its citizens continue to enjoy one of the highest standards of living in the world.

Two opposing points of view on the question of Québec independence: the top poster asks: "Separation? You're right to say NO"; the bottom poster counters with a big "YES" because, it says, "it will become possible."

Almanac

POLITICAL

Country name:
Official form: Canada
Short form: none
Local official form: Canada
Local short form: none

Nationality:
    noun: Canadian
    adjective: Canadian

Official languages: English and French

Capital city: Ottawa

Type of government: constitutional monarchy, federal state, and parliamentary democracy

Suffrage (voting rights): everyone 18 years and over

Overseas territories: none

National anthem: "O Canada" (English and French versions)

National day: July 1 (Canada Day)

Flag:

GEOGRAPHICAL

Location: North America; latitudes 42° to 84° north and longitudes 53° to 141° west.

Climate: ranges from Arctic and sub-arctic (north) to cool (south)

Total area: 3,851,790 square miles (9,976,136 sq. km)
Land: 92%
Water: 8%

Coastline: 152,110 miles (244,790 km)

Terrain: Mountainous regions to the north, east, and west rim a basinlike inland.

Highest point: Mount Logan, 19,850 feet (6,050 m)
Lowest point: Atlantic Ocean, 0 feet (0 m)

Natural resources: coal, oil, natural gas, gold, zinc, uranium, wood, and hydroelectric power

Land use (1993 est.):
    arable land: 5%
    forests and woodland: 54%
    meadows and pasture: 3%

permanent crops: 0%

other: 38%

Natural hazards and obstacles:
Permafrost covers the north,
hindering development;
cyclonic storms form east
of the Rocky Mountains.

POPULATION

Population (1998): 30.7 million

Population growth rate (1998 est.):
1.09%

Birth rate (1997 est.): 12.12 births
per 1,000 of the population

Death rate (1997 est.): 7.25 deaths
per 1,000 of the population

Sex ratio (1997 est.): 98 males per
100 females

Total fertility rate (1998 est.):
165 children born for every
1,000 females

Infant mortality rate (1998 est.):
5.59 deaths per 1,000 live births

Life expectancy at birth (1998 est.):
total population: 79.16 years
male: 75.86 years
female: 82.63 years

Literacy (1996 est.):
total population: 99%
male: 99%
female: 99%

ECONOMY

Currency: Canadian dollar (C$);
1 C$ = 100 cents

Exchange rate (1999):
$1 = 1.4 C$

Gross national product (GNP) (1996):
$570 billion (ninth-largest
economy in the world)

Average annual growth rate
(1990–1996): 1.9%

GNP per capita (1997 est.): $21,700

Average annual inflation rate
(1990–1997): 2.4%

Unemployment rate (1999): 8%

Exports (1996): $205.8 billion
Imports (1996): $175.7 billion

Foreign aid given (1995): $1.6 billion

Human Development Index:
(an index scaled from 0 to 100 combining statistics
indicating adult literacy, years of schooling, life
expectancy, and income levels within a country):
96.0 (U.S. 94.2)

TIME LINE—CANADA

World History

Canadian History

c. 30,000 B.C.

c. 40,000 Modern humans—*Homo sapiens sapiens*—emerge.

The first Native American peoples arrive in North America from Asia.

c. 3000 B.C.

c. 2500 Ancient Egyptians build the pyramids and Sphinx in Giza.

The Inuit people arrive in North America.

c. A.D. 1000

1000 French king Charlemagne is crowned Emperor of the Western Empire in Europe.

1000 Viking Leif Eriksson lands in Vinland, a name he gives to a site in what is now Newfoundland.

c. 1500

1492 Columbus arrives in America—Europe begins period of exploration and colonization.

1497 John Cabot claims Newfoundland for England.

1534 Jacques Cartier explores St. Lawrence River and claims the area for France.

1620 Pilgrims land in New England.

c. 1600

1670 Hudson Bay Company founded and granted trading rights in much of central and eastern Canada.

1608 Samuel de Champlain founds Habitation de Québec (later Québec City).

c. 1700

1789 The French Revolution begins.

1775 The American Revolution begins.

1774 The Quebec Act grants French Canadians political and religious rights.

1763 France finally surrenders New France to Britain.

c. 1800

1837 Queen Victoria ascends the throne of Britain.

Europe begins to industrialize.

1812 U.S. declares war on Britain, and many battles are fought in Canada.

c. 1850

1859 Charles Darwin publishes *Origin of Species*.
1861–1865 American Civil War.

1867 Nova Scotia, New Brunswick, Québec, and Ontario form the Confederation of Canada.

1870 The Red River Rebellion breaks out.

2000 The West celebrates the Millennium— 2,000 years since the birth of Christ.

1999 The Inuit territory of Nunavut is established.

1995 Slightly more than 50 percent of Québecois vote for Québec to remain part of Canada.

c. 1900

1914–1918 World War I.

1917 Revolution brings communism to Russia.

1896 The Klondike Gold Rush begins.

1905 Saskatchewan and Alberta become Canadian provinces.

1918 Women gain the right to vote.

1989 The Berlin Wall falls, as communism crumbles in Eastern Europe.

c. 2000

1989 Canada and the U.S. sign Free Trade Agreement.

1980 Québec holds its first referendum on separation from Canada. A large majority votes to remain with Canada.

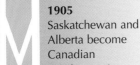

c. 1930

1929 Worldwide economic downturn begins.

1939–1945 World War II.

1931 Canada wins full independence from Britain.

1939 Canada declares war on Germany.

1949 Newfoundland becomes Canada's tenth province.

1973 The Vietnam War ends.

1969 The first man lands on the moon.

c. 1980

1970 Québec separatists kidnap and kill Pierre Laporte, Québec's minister of labor.

1950 Inuit people gain right to vote in federal elections.

c. 1950

Glossary

Abbreviations:
Fr. = French
Nat. = Native North
     American Language

Allies: The nations that joined to fight against Germany and its associates during World Wars I and II, including Great Britain, France, the United States, Canada, and Russia.

anglophone: Term used to describe Canadian people whose mother tongue is English.

archipelago: A chain of islands.

aurora borealis: Atmospheric phenomenon of shifting lights in the sky.

Canadiens (**Fr.**): French inhabitants of Canada in colonial times.

chanson d'aviron (**Fr.**): A rowing song of *voyageurs*.

chinook: Warm westerly wind that occasionally comes off the eastern slopes of the Rocky Mountains during the winter months.

confederation: The formation of a nation through the union of separate states that share common interests.

coniferous: Cone bearing.

constitution: The fundamental principles that underlie the government of a country.

coureur du bois (**Fr. "wood-runners"**): The fur traders of New France; also known as *voyageurs*.

crustacean: An invertebrate (spineless) animal with hard outer shell and segmented body that usually lives in water; for example, crabs, lobsters, and shrimp.

exports: Goods sold by one country to another.

First Nations: The first inhabitants of Canada; Native North Americans. The Inuit, who arrived in America much later, are not included among the First Nations.

fleur-de-lys: A stylized lily and the traditional symbol of French royalty.

francophone: Term used to describe Canadians whose mother tongue is French.

Great Depression: Period of widespread economic slowdown that followed the Wall Street Crash of 1929; characterized by inflation, unemployment, and poverty.

gross national product (GNP): The total value of goods and services produced by a nation during a period, usually a year.

habitants (**Fr.**): Tenant farmers who worked the land belonging to *seigneurs*.

Haida: Native people whose traditional homelands are the Queen Charlotte Islands, British Columbia.

hydroelectricity: Electricity produced by harnessing the water power in rivers.

igloo: A domed, ice-block dwelling made by the Inuit.

imports: Goods bought by one country from another.

Inuit: Native people of Arctic Canada, Alaska, and Greenland.

joual (**Fr.**): French dialect spoken in Québec that combines French, English words, and slang.

kanata (**Nat.**): Iroquois word for "village," from which the name "Canada" probably derives.

komitak (**Nat.**): An Inuit dog sled.

Kwakwaka'wakw: Native people whose traditional homelands are the present-day Vancouver Island and the coast of British Columbia.

Métis: Native people of mixed French and Native descent.

Mi'kmaq (or Micmac): Native people whose traditional homelands lie in present-day Nova Scotia.

Mountie: A member of the Royal Canadian Mounted Police.

Native: Term used to describe any of the first inhabitants of Canada.

North Atlantic Treaty Organization (NATO): Mutual defense pact made up of Western nations including the United States, Canada, and Great Britain.

Pacific Rim: Economic and political term used to describe countries that border the Pacific—including Japan, Australia, Canada, Thailand.

parliament: A nation's law-making (legislative) body.

peninsula: Finger of land that stretches out into the sea.

permafrost: Permanently frozen subsoil.

potlatch (Nat. "gift"): Native ceremony held to improve the host's status.

Québécois: The version of French spoken in Québec; an inhabitant of Québec.

referendum: National vote on an important issue.

seigneur **(Fr.):** French army officer who was granted land in the colony of New France.

state, the: The government of a country or nation.

subarctic: Regions immediately south of the Arctic Circle.

taiga: Zone of coniferous forests south of the tundra.

tundra: Treeless, marshy plains of the Arctic region.

umiak **(Nat.):** Inuit canoe that may hold up to 20 people.

voyageurs **(Fr.):** The fur traders of New France; also known as *coureurs du bois*.

World Heritage Site: Buildings, landscapes, or archaeological sites designated to be of universal cultural value by the United Nations (UNESCO).

Bibliography

Major Sources Used for This Book

Brown, R.C., ed. *The Illustrated History of Canada*. Toronto: Lester Publishing, 1998

McMillan, A.D. *Native Peoples and Cultures of Canada*. Vancouver: Douglas & MacIntyre, 1997.

McNaught, K. *The Penguin History of Canada*. New York: Penguin, 1991.

Oxford Companion to Canadian Literature. Oxford: OUP, 1983.

Woodcock, G. *A Social History of Canada*. New York: Penguin, 1989.

General Further Reading

The DK Geography of the World. New York: Dorling Kindersley, 1996.

The Kingfisher History Encyclopedia. New York: Kingfisher, 1999.

Student Atlas. New York: Dorling Kindersley, 1998.

Further Reading About Canada

Canada Through the Decades (ten-volume series). Calgary: Weigl Educational Publishers, 1999–2000.

Great Canadians (ten-volume series). Calgary: Weigl Educational Publishers, 1999–2000.

Berton, P. *Adventures in Canadian History* (series). Toronto: McClelland and Stewart, 1996.

Davis, P., ed. *The History Atlas of North America*. Foster City: IDG Books, 1998.

Younkin, P., and A. Hirschfelder. *Indians of the Arctic and Subarctic*. New York: Facts on File, 1992.

Some Websites About Canada

Teaching and Learning about Canada— www3.ns.sympatico.ca/manbenn/teach.htm

Welcome to Nunavut—www.inac.gc.ca/ nunavut/Nunavut/Welcome.html

Index

Acknowledgments

Cover Photo Credits
Bruce Coleman: The Purcell Team (background);
Tony Stone Images: Kevin Miller (crest poles); **Peter**
Newark's American Pictures (*coureur du bois*)

Photo Credits
AKG London: 96; **Bridgeman Art Library:** Art
Gallery of Ontario, Toronto 98; **Bruce Coleman:**
Wayne Lankinen 28; **Corbis:** Gary Braasch 6; Yves
Debay 118; Kevin Fleming 108; Lowell Georgia 71;
Philip Gould 61; Annie Griffiths Belt 84; Peter
Harholdt 100, 104; Wolfgang Kaehler 22, 91;
Kelly-Mooney Photography 40; Earl Kowall 74, 119;
Gunter Marx 79, 110; The Purcell Team 94; Joel W.
Rogers 80; Joseph Sohm: ChromoSohn Inc 89; Paul
Souders 34, 47; Staffan Widstrand 29, 92; **ET**
Archive: Viking Ship Museum, Oslo 53; **Mary Evans**
Picture Library: 52, 54, 55, 56, 58, 63, 67;
Hutchison Library: Robert Francis 106; Trevor Page
25; Bernard Regent 35, 38; **Image Bank:** Joseph Van
Os 17; **Image Bank/Archive Photos:** Frank Driggs
103; Bernard Gotfryd 90; Sporting News 115; **Peter**
Newark's American Pictures: 48, 59, 114; **Redferns:**
James Dittinger 105; **Rex Features:** 101; **Tony Stone**
Images: James Balog 31; Wayne R. Bilenduke 26,
116; Cosmo Condina 14; Nicholas DeVore 23; John
Edwards 42; Suzanne and Nick Geary 19; Chris
Johns 87; Kevin Miller 50; David E. Myers 30; Frank
Oberle 27; Stefan Schulhof 45; Ed Simpson 20; Alan
Smith 77; Robin Smith 24; Art Wolfe 12.

WITHDRAWN